D1015846

HOME RUN HERO

- Ever since he set the rookie record in1987 with 49 home runs, Mark McGwire has been a crowd favorite. Fans love to watch his awe-inspiring home runs.
- Big Mac set the record for the first player ever to hit over 50 home runs in three consecutive seasons.
- Going, going, gone! On September 8, 1998, Mark McGwire blasted his 62nd home run, breaking the most famous of baseball's records: the 61 home runs hit by Roger Maris in 1961.

Here's Mark McGwire, from his early years in little league, to his starring role as a major-league home run record-breaker. Read all about the incredibly popular and respected first baseman who will go down in history as a true baseball legend.

MARK McGWIRE
A Biography

MARK McGWIRE

A Biography

JONATHAN HALL

AN ARCHWAY PAPERBACK
Published by POCKET BOOKS
New York London Toronto Sydney Tokyo Singapore

AN ARCHWAY PAPERBACK *Original*

An Archway Paperback published by
POCKET BOOKS, a division of Simon & Schuster Inc.
1230 Avenue of the Americas, New York, NY 10020

ISBN: 0-671-03273-9

First Archway Paperback printing November 1998

10 9 8 7 6 5 4 3 2 1

AN ARCHWAY PAPERBACK and colophon are
registered trademarks of Simon & Schuster Inc.

Front cover photo by Larry Marano/ULM/London Features
International, inset photo by Rob Tringali Jr./Sportschrome USA

Printed in the U.S.A.

IL: 7

To my mom,
DOROTHY C. HALL

Acknowledgments

I would like to acknowledge Karen and Scott; my dog, Clyde; and especially Julie, who has taught me everything I know about baseball.

· 1 ·

SAVING BASEBALL

The most compelling aspect of any sporting event is the natural unfolding of a plotline in which nobody knows the ending. Each and every game has the equal chance to be a snoozer or a classic, usually falling somewhere in between.

Likewise, an athletic performer never knows if he or she will be the hero or the goat until that split second when there exists the opportunity to affect the outcome of a competition. Occasionally, there comes a player who wins a large share of games, becoming a hero more often than a goat. Even rarer is there the performer who regularly does something magical.

Mark McGwire is such a player.

It was on a lazy Sunday evening in late August when Mr. McGwire was presented an opportunity to perform some magic of his own. It was the kind of night when people realize that the end of summer has suddenly sneaked up much sooner than expected. The kind of evening where you kick your feet up and quietly watch whatever sporting event happens to be on television.

On this specific evening, however, there was a competition occurring that was of particular interest to baseball fans across the country. This, of course, was the race for the most sacred record in the revered heritage of the nation's pastime—the battle to break Roger Maris's 37-year-old record of 61 home runs in a single season. Chicago Cubs outfielder Sammy Sosa had just tied his competitor earlier in the afternoon in Denver's Coors Field against the Colorado Rockies with his 54th home run. As fate would have it, the individual that Sosa had been chasing just happened to be playing an evening game that Sunday—a game that was to be nationally televised on ESPN's *Sunday Night Baseball* program. Many Americans were tuned in that evening to see St. Louis Cardinals first baseman Mark McGwire chase history. Particularly they wanted to see how he would respond to Sosa's tying home run.

The Cardinals were playing host to undoubtedly the best team in the National League—the Atlanta Braves. While the Braves were certain to win their division and go to the playoffs, the Cardinals were not as successful, having played just under .500 baseball since early May. Despite the fact that this game would have little impact on the post seasons of either team, the stadium was filled to capacity with fans who were there to witness history. Each fan knew that there was a good chance they would see a home run hit by their hometown hero, Mark McGwire, who was on a pace to smash the hallowed home run record set by Maris a distant 37 years earlier.

The game was an uneven affair, with the Braves jumping out to a 6–0 lead after three quick innings. Every time Mark would step to the plate, the crowd seemingly held their collective breath in hopes of seeing the monstrous first baseman hit his 55th home run. In his first three at bats, Big Mac walked, hit a single, then a double, scoring twice to bring the Cards closer to the Braves. Going into the bottom of the seventh inning, the Cardinals trailed, 7–5.

The St. Louis faithful were relieved to see Mark stroke the ball with confidence again as they were all aware of the minislump he had recently been mired in. Big Mac had not hit one out of the park since the previous Wednesday, and it did not help that the home plate umpire had ejected him in the first inning of the previous game (for arguing balls and strikes). With Sammy Sosa tying Mac's 54th earlier in the day, McGwire and his loyal legion of fans were eager for home run 55.

With teammates Delino DeShields and

Brian Jordan on base, Big Mac came to the plate to face the Braves' veteran reliever Dennis Martinez. Virtually every baseball fan in America had tuned in to watch Mark McGwire do some magic and here was a golden opportunity. After McGuire took the first pitch high and away, the television commentator predicted that Martinez would be very careful in placing pitches outside the strike zone. After all, a walk would be a lot better to the Braves than a home run—McGwire's specialty. On the second pitch, the Braves' reliever let go a meaty fastball right over the middle of the plate.

Mark McGwire pounced.

Home run number 55.

Cardinals 8, Braves 7.

The fans in Busch Stadium went crazy.

Every fan watching that game on television that night let out a little whoop of surprised glee when Mac tagged that pitch—sending it a whopping *500 feet!* Not only had Big Mac responded to the pressure of the particular game situation, winning the game with a 3-run shot. Mr. McGwire was also making a statement to anyone who doubted his ability and strength of character to set and keep pace on his home run chase.

After the game, Mac was asked how he felt about "it."

"What? The win?" he said with a smile. He knew that the mass of reporters that were in the postgame press conference were there to discuss the home run record and not the game. But in a self-effacing manner that has become his trademark, McGwire deflected the praise he was receiving about his home runs. "It feels good to come back and win a game, feels even better doing it against one of the best teams in the National League," he said.

He didn't comment about his physical accomplishment. He didn't boast or talk trash to his home run rival. Rather he used the opportunity to discredit the competitive hype that the media was creating, offering, "I don't see the homer thing as a challenge between me and Sammy." He added, "What a great year, what a historical year. Wouldn't that be something if both Sammy and me hit—what is it 62 or 63 homers each?"

"I'm excited for Sammy. He's having a magical year. Way better than I am having. He's got a higher batting average, he's driven in more runs, and his team is in the race for the wild card in the playoffs." These quotes typify what is most exceptional about Mark McGwire. Not his awesome show of power, his concentration, or his ability to hit home runs. The characteristic that has made Mark McGwire a hero to so many is the respect he shows his friends, fans, and competitors, as well as the pure class in which he deals with everyone around him.

If an athlete is judged by his performance on the field, he is liked and accepted as much by his performance off the field. In 1998, Mark McGwire set himself apart from all other professional athletes. He did this not only in his tireless pursuit of one of baseball's most hallowed records. Mark McGwire's behavior throughout the season set a standard from which all others could learn.

But it had not always been like this. Mark had endured numerous ups and downs throughout his personal and professional life that gave him the proper perspective in which he could view the world around him. He had, on a few occasions, taken pause to reflect on all that was going on both within and around him. He had learned to build on his already strong character through hardship and adversity. He had looked for the support from his loving family, friends, and teammates.

And from all this experience, Mark McGwire developed a terrific understanding of how to accomplish his ultimate goal—breaking the single-season record of 61 home runs.

There is nothing quite as majestic, awe-inspiring, and pure as a home run. It is not a statistical equation, like a batting average.

It is a simple feat of athletic prowess—a batter hits the ball over the fence. Without question, there is no other sports achievement that captivates the imagination and fantasy of its fans more than the single-season home run record. Babe Ruth held the record at 60 since 1927, then Roger Maris broke it in 1961 with 61. Since then, it was a record that seemed to be etched in stone, with no one making a serious run at that venerable mark.

Until 1998, the season that saved baseball.

GROWING UP McGWIRE

There are many families across this country that are just like the McGwires. A middle-class, suburban family of five children is actually fairly common across the globe. However, there was something particular about the McGwire household that enabled Mark to excel in athletics. There was also something very special in the way in which the McGwire children were raised—respect, gratitude, and hard work were the cornerstones of the McGwire household. These principles were taught by John and Ginger McGwire (Mark's parents) because they had experienced their own set of victories and hardships themselves. And, as is the case in most families, the basis of a child's rearing comes from a parent's own point of view.

It was 1944 when a seven-year-old John McGwire (Mark's father) walked across the floor of his family's house, when suddenly his legs "just gave way" and he collapsed. Young John's stepfather called the doctor, who eventually gave him very difficult news—John had polio. Since a vaccine for this disease had not yet been discovered, John was taken to a special contagious-patients ward of the local hospital, where he was allowed absolutely no visitors. There he stayed for six months, without a visit even from his mother. Everyday, his bed would be rolled to the window where he could see his loving family and wave longingly at his mother and stepdad.

Eventually, John became healthy enough to leave the hospital, but the dangerous disease left one leg significantly shorter than the other. Despite this disability, John remained positive and went on to be a fiery competitor and active in many different sports.

It was this positive outlook and overcoming of adversity that taught the McGwire children that they could accomplish whatever they set their minds to.

To say the McGwire household was athletic would be an understatement. John was an avid golfer, an amateur boxer, and an enthusiastic cyclist—he once biked 400 miles on one camping trip. One of Mark's earliest memories was the rat-a-tat-tat of a speed bag echoing in the garage as his dad pounded away. An accomplished high school varsity swimmer, Ginger (Mark's mother) was also quite athletic. She understood the mindset of a competitor and later was always there to both support and teach respect to her sons. John and Ginger were married and bought a house in a nice little cul-de-sac in Claremont, California. They proceeded to have five healthy children. All are boys. All are huge. All are extremely athletic.

The cul-de-sac where the McGwires grew up became the scene of many neighborhood games and activities. Mark and his friends would often chalk-out sidelines and play Nerf football or tennis baseball for hours on end.

Mark was the sort of kid who participated in a sport every season simply because there was little else to do. "Golf was the first game I learned," he told a writer. "My dad taught me how to grip a club when I was five, and I never had another lesson." Mark became a very good golfer. Of course, it isn't difficult to imagine that the same frame that can hammer a baseball 500-plus feet is also capable of driving a golf ball 350 yards.

Mark started playing baseball when he was eight years old in a casual youth league. At that time, Mark was already much bigger and stronger than his team-mates and was much more interested in pitching than hitting or playing the field. When Mark turned ten, he joined a better-organized and more official Little League program. It was the sort of league where teams had fancy uniforms, and the level of competition was considerably better than his previous league. In Mark's first at bat he was admittedly nervous. But he believed in himself mightily and took a pitch he thought looked good. With his eyes closed, he felt his bat meet the ball with a loud crack. Mark opened his eyes to see the soaring arc of a ball destined to land on the home run side of the outfield fence. Mark suddenly enjoyed hitting a whole lot more.

Still, golf was Mark's first love, and he wanted to get back to it. When he was a sophomore in high school, Mark actually quit the baseball team to concentrate on golf. "I had pulled a chest muscle, so it would be a while before I could really swing a bat," he said. "I had been playing on the junior-varsity [baseball] team, which didn't excite me much. I'd been playing golf for years.

"The thing I liked about golf was that you were the only one there to blame when something went wrong." Mark was successful on the golf course. When he was 15, he

ard worker. And I liked to do a lot of
where people couldn't see me. I'd
balls against a cement wall or set a
a tee and hit it."

work paid off. As a senior at Damien
School, Mark had an impressive bat-
average of .359 and 5 home runs. He
boasted an earned run average of 1.90
a won-lost record of 5–3 as a pitcher.
would be good enough to garner the
ntion of the head coaches at both
zona State University and the University
Southern California. Mark visited both
lleges, excited by the opportunity to play
aseball at the college level. But before he
got too far in that direction, the Montreal
Expos drafted him out of high school.
Suddenly, his decision for the future
became a lot bigger.

Professional baseball was now a realistic
opportunity. But was Mark really ready to
forgo a free college education to play minor
league baseball? Fortunately, the Expos
made Mark's decision a lot easier by offer-

shot a personal-best round of 72 to tie for
the tournament lead, sending Mark and his
opponent to a sudden-death playoff.
Though he and his opponent remained tied
throughout the first four extra holes, Mark
sank a birdie putt on the fifth playoff hole
to win the tournament and earn his first
victory on the golf course. Still, Mark
missed baseball, and he eventually went
back to it.

Because of his physical presence, Mark
was typically placed in positions in which
he would make the most significant impact.
When Mark wasn't pitching, he would be
playing shortstop, and he would almost
always hit in the cleanup spot. John often
received comments from coaches and parents about Mark's natural ability and how
well suited his son was for the major
leagues. But Mark never paid too much
attention to those comments. In fact, he and
his friends would all later admit that they
were playing simply for fun. They didn't pay
a whole lot of attention to the majors, and

none of them ever thought that Mark would one day be a pro, let alone a star.

"As parents, we never gloated over Mark's success," John McGwire told an interviewer. "Even when some of the city's old time ballplayers and opposing Little League coaches would stop and tell me that Mark was a future big leaguer, I never let him know about it." Mark's mother told another reporter, "I've never felt that Mark was ever as impressed with his success in sports as other people. Aware of it yes, but never big headed about it. I've always assumed that we were like most families—that we tried to teach our kids the importance of always doing their best, being polite, and respecting other people." It isn't difficult to see how Mark learned about humility and respect.

As Mark's success on the baseball diamond became more commonplace, he learned many valuable lessons. In one particularly difficult outing on the pitching mound, Mark was so upset with himself for

walking so many batter
ing on the mound *durin*
the coach of the team,
places with the shortstop.
got in position, something
can still remember looking
from shortstop, and everyt
fuzzy," Mark says. "I got glas
that."

Mark's improved eyesight
benefit to his overall game. His s
tinued. In fact, while playing a
Upland, a Los Angeles suburb, M
ball over the fence and across th
The street just happened to be the
between Los Angeles and San Bern
counties. Mark had hit the ball into an
county!

Despite his on-the-field exploits, Ma
remained a quiet and shy individual. "I wa
always the kind of kid who liked to sit in the
back of the room and just blend in," Mark
once told a sportswriter. "I was always just a
basic athlete, nothing extraordinary. But I

ing a contract that was not very attractive. "I'd never thought of going to college because I didn't think I'd enjoy it," Mark would later say about choosing to attend the University of Southern California. "That was one of the best decisions I've ever made."

...

· 3 ·

MAKING THE MAJORS

Chief among the reasons why
Mark chose to play collegiate
baseball at the University of
Southern California were
head coach Rod Dedeaux and pitching coach
Marcel Lachemann. Respected by his coaching peers and former players alike, the list of
professional players that Coach Dedeaux has
coached at the college level is long. Fred
Lynn, Tom Seaver, Steve Kemp, and Dave
Kingman are all USC graduates who went on
to enjoy long and successful professional
careers. Mark McGwire had a lot in common
with two of these players. According to
Coach Dedeaux, "Most good athletes are
either pitchers or shortstops in high school.

Fred Lynn came to USC as a pitcher; so did Dave Kingman."

When Mark arrived at USC, he, too, was most interested in pitching. As a freshman, he was used rather sparingly, appearing in 29 games—20 as a pitcher. His ERA of 3.04 was a lot more impressive than his batting average of .200 in 75 at bats.

After his freshman year, Mark was shocked to learn that Coach Lachemann (the pitching coach who had primarily recruited him) was leaving to take a coaching job in the minors. So when Coach Lachemann left, so did Mark's love of pitching.

Mark spent the following summer in the Alaska Summer League with Trojan assistant coach Ron Vaughn. Many writers over the last ten years have pointed to this experience as crucial in Mac's development as a hitter. Mark played first base exclusively for the summer-league team, leading them to the National Baseball Congress finals, held in Wichita, Kansas each year.

As Mark's college career progressed, he continued to put up impressive numbers. In a strange bit of foreshadowing, Mark found himself caught up in a home run–record chase during his sophomore season. The single-season mark was 17 dingers, and Mac was on a pace to break that record by a long shot. Mark was way ahead of the pace when he hit his 17th home run, tying the record with several games left. He just needed to belt one more out of the park, and the record was his. Unfortunately, Mark was unaccustomed to the pressure and promptly went into a slump over the next seven games. Finally, Mark hit a line-drive shot over the center-field fence and broke the USC single-season home run record. He would later add another dinger, totaling 19 for the season (which happens to be much shorter than the professional season).

The rest of Mark's career at Southern Cal was balanced. Not only was Mark hitting many balls over the fences, he was hitting for average as well. While his fielding improved significantly at first base, Mark was not convinced that he would find a spot in the professional leagues and there-fore was majoring in public administration as a backup plan. He always felt that a career as a policeman would have suited him well.

Mark's junior year kept him from gradu-ating and pursing his career as a civil ser-vant, for it was this year that Mark bested his own single-season home run record by hitting 32 round-trippers in one season. Not only did he set school and conference records, but he attracted a great deal of attention from professional scouts as well. With the type of season Mac was playing, there was little question that he would enjoy a high draft position in the major league draft.

Baseball America is generally regarded as the premier scouting journal for profes-sional scouts. In its report on Mark McGwire it said: ". . . most scouting directors agree that he is the leading power-hitting prospect available in the draft." Still, there were those who had their doubts. It was unclear how high Mac would go in the draft.

The New York Mets had the first pick in the 1984 draft. Head scout Joe McIlvaine would later report that they were ready to make Mark McGwire the first pick of the draft, but they were not convinced that Mark would sign with the Mets organization. They were ultimately dissuaded and chose a little-known high school player named Shawn Abner with whom they were also particularly enamored. Unfortunately, Shawn Abner never developed into an outstanding major-league player.

When the draft started, nine picks went by without Mark McGwire's name being announced. Finally, the Oakland General Manager, Sandy Alderson, made the selection. Mark McGwire was chosen in the first round of the 1984 draft with the tenth pick overall. Mark was going to be a part of the Oakland Athletics organization. He was thrilled.

Before Mark was to enter the Athletics farm system, he was given the opportunity to participate in the 1984 Olympics. Baseball had never been an Olympic event, and though technically only a demonstration event, this would be the first time that America's pastime would be a part of the Olympic tradition.

Because of the Soviet-bloc boycott of the 1984 games, Cuba would not be participating, and therefore the hometown Team USA was the heavy favorite to bring home the gold. The talent collected on that team comprised perhaps the best amateur American team ever put together. The U.S. team had relatively few problems getting to the gold-medal game against an outmatched Japanese team. Unfortunately, the Americans overlooked their Far Eastern foe, ultimately losing the game, 6–3, and the gold medal. Mark still looks at this loss with a bit of confusion. There was so much more talent on the U.S. team, he can't understand how they lost.

Instead of focusing on the Olympic loss, Mark packed his belongings and reported to the Athletics farm club in Modesto, California. While it was only the minor leagues, Mark was excited to be there. Unfortunately, his enthusiasm did not translate to immediate success on the field. A slow start is not unusual for a ballplayer making the transition from the college ranks to the pros, primarily due to the adjustment of going from an aluminum bat to a wooden one.

The Oakland farm system was loaded with talent at that time. Among the other players that were ready to be called up to the majors were Jose Canseco, Eric Plunk, Walt Weiss, Tim Belcher, Luis Polonia, and Stan Javier—all extremely successful major-league players in their own right. So Mac was not short on competition and was eager to get to the majors. Soon he was hitting the ball (with a wooden bat) just as he had done throughout his career. Home runs were flying off of his bat as his batting average continued to rise.

Slowly but surely, Mark made the leap from the Single-A training league to the Double-A team in Huntsville, Alabama. The jump to Double-A is thought by most scouts to be the most difficult transition for all baseball prospects. The level of competition is significantly higher, as this is truly the first proving ground for major-league prospects. Mac succeeded at this level, and it was not long before he was promoted to Triple-A in Tacoma, Washington. While there, Mark hit an impressive .351, hitting 9 home runs and driving in a total of 29 runs.

On August 20, Mark was brought into the Tacoma manager's office for some important news. Mark was being sent to the majors. He was ready. He flew to Baltimore to join his new teammates for a series with the Orioles. Unfortunately for Mark, Mother Nature would not be on his side, with the entire series being rained out. Oh well, on to New York.

It was Friday night, August 22, 1986. Mark McGwire's first major league game, in baseball's most hallowed ground—Yankee Stadium.

Mark's first two games were forgettable— going 0-for-3 in each game. However, in his third game, facing family friend Tommy John on the mound, Mark went off, collecting the first three hits of his major-league career in a 11–4 Oakland win. Mark was beginning to feel comfortable in this place.

Typically, major-league ball clubs bring their top talent from their farm system up to the major leagues at the end of the season, especially when a team is no longer involved in a race for the playoffs. Such was the case with Mark McGwire and the slew of other talented players who had come up from the farm system. Mark knew that he could succeed at this level and dedicated the remainder of the season to focusing and working on his game.

Looking around him, Mark was impressed with both the talent and camaraderie he noticed with this collection of ballplayers. Technically, the following year would be his rookie year in the major leagues. He had a good feeling about it.

ROOKIE OF THE YEAR

As spring training for the 1987 season began, Mark McGwire knew that he would have to work very hard to play a significant amount of time for the Oakland Athletics and not be relegated to the Triple-A ball club in Tacoma. A 40-year-old Hall of Famer by the name of Reggie Jackson was also participating that year, in hopes of making one last comeback with the team where he had began his career roughly 17 years earlier. Reggie had promised himself to be the hardest-working individual in camp that year, and his tireless workouts and additional laps proved his extra effort. But A's manager Tony La Russa noticed another player who was keeping right up with Reggie. Tony knew that the A's had something special when he saw the effort that the young rookie first baseman was putting forth. He was impressed with Mark McGwire.

The hard work in spring training coincided with a strong performance at the plate. Mark hit a very strong .322 and led his team with 32 RBIs, earning himself a spot on the opening-day roster of the Oakland A's. However, Coach La Russa could not decide who to play at first base on a regular basis, Mac or another impressive rookie named Rob Nelson. Because both exhibited a lot of potential, it was decided that the two rookies would split time at first base, Mark would start in games against left-handed pitchers, and Rob would start against right-handers. This strategy is called "platooning" and is often used to exploit the supposed advantage that a batter has in facing the opposite-handed pitcher. Since Mark batted from the right side of the plate, it made sense that he would only face lefties.

In the first few weeks of action, neither Rob nor Mark was too impressive at the plate. Mr. Nelson struck out in 12 of his first 24 at bats, and Mr. McGwire was hitting a paltry .167 with only 1 home run. Coach LaRussa could see that the lack of experience was actually a detriment to the development of both players and decided to go with one, full-time first baseman. Because Mark seemed to be making more consistent and aggressive cuts at the ball, Tony gave the starting spot to Mac, sending Rob Nelson down to the minors. While Mac's confidence grew with that decision, he didn't exactly set the stadium on fire with his hot hitting in the month of April. However, he did hit three more home runs, finishing the month with a total of four round-trippers.

As the month of May began, Mark started to get into a groove with his swing. He went with that feeling at the plate and began to tear the cover off the ball. Not only was he seeing the ball come across the plate very well, he was often watching the ball sail over the outfield fences. In a three-game series at Detroit's Tiger Stadium, Mark hit 5 home runs. Over a 16-game span, he hit 11 dingers. Mark owned the month of May, finishing with 15 four-baggers for the month, 1 short of the major-league record for most home runs in a month, 16, held by Mickey Mantle.

Combined with the 4 that he had hit in April, suddenly this big, red-headed rookie found himself atop the home run leaders. It was at this point that the national media really began to take notice. Here was a 23-year-old rookie who was hitting home runs like the venerable Babe Ruth himself. This was a great story, sure to sell a lot of newspapers and magazines. One article specifically tried to give Mark a slick nickname, marketable to the masses. Some of the suggestions were funny: Orange Crunch, Marco Solo, and the McG Force. The coverage was very positive, although Mac's little-boy shyness was still very much alive. Mark didn't quite know exactly how to deal with all of the attention, so he decided to be as natural as possible and just go with the flow.

By the time the All-Star Game had rolled around, McGwire had smashed 33 homers in just over half the season. He was the first rookie ever to hit the 30 mark before the All-Star break and the first to hit 5 homers in a two-game set. He was also on a pace to easily surpass the rookie home run record of 38 held by Frank Robinson and Wally Berger. Some were even talking that Mac would come close to challenging Roger Maris's single season record of 61, although the columnists and commentators who knew baseball best disagreed, calling it "virtually impossible" for a rookie to break such a historic record. At any rate, Mark's power was rewarded with a prestigious reserve role on the American League All-Star team.

Mark didn't pay much heed to all the attention he was getting, focusing instead on his overall baseball game. The media picked up on Mark's humble spirit as well as his strong work ethic and liked him even more. A *Sports Illustrated* article made this point by retelling an interaction between Mark and Reggie Jackson from back when Mac was touring with the U.S. Olympic Team. After watching Mac crank a shot 450 feet to dead center, Reggie pulled the young man aside and said, "Son, when you hit a ball like that, you've got to watch it." Mark replied, "No, that's not my style."

Regarding all the media attention he was suddenly getting, Mark said, "It's pretty neat. I don't do anything special, just concentrate, see the ball, hit the ball, and be aggressive." When asked about his particularly strong start as an individual, Mark replied, "I'm really enjoying the way we're playing as a team."

He was too good to be true! Here was a young kid that had all the opportunity to beat his chest and showboat. Instead, he was respectful, humble, and nice. Suddenly, Mark's face was everywhere—the new home run king!

Mac was not the only talented player on this Oakland team. In fact, the A's were putting together quite a successful year, staying within a few games of the division-leading Kansas City Royals throughout most of the season. It was truly a great time to be an A's fan.

Mark had a little help in dealing with life as a rookie sensation. His teammate, Jose Canseco, had put together a terrific season the previous year, hitting 33 home runs himself, earning Rookie-of-the-Year honors. Jose's build (and style of game) was very similar to Mac's. They were both big men who showed a propensity for hitting the long ball. As such, marketing gurus labeled the two the Bash Brothers, modeled after the Blues Brothers. The Athletics' chief division rivals could not believe Oakland's good fortune, Jose Canseco and Mark McGwire joining their team in consecutive years.

After the All-Star Game, Mark continued his torrid pace, finishing the month of July with a total of 37 home runs. The month of August was much slower, however, as Mark didn't tie the single-season home run record for rookies until the 11th. He broke the record three games later in Anaheim Stadium in California, not far from where he grew up. Mark would only hit 1 more home run in the month of August, finishing with a total of 40 heading into September. The earlier talk of approaching the Maris record of 61 was no longer relevant.

Mark would later explain to a reporter that all of the press coverage did affect his playing style in the month of August. He told *Inside Sports*, "It bothered me. It affected my concentration because I couldn't get in the right frame of mind. I had never thought much about records, but there was always someone there to remind me of them. First it was the rookie home run record, and then it was Ruth and Maris. It put pressure on me that I hadn't put on myself. I had a bad August, and I know that was the reason."

While talk of breaking records subsided a bit, many in the press realized that no rookie had ever hit 50 home runs in a single season. In fact, only 11 players in the history of baseball *ever* hit as many. Suddenly there was a new target for Mac. Meanwhile, Mark and his teammates didn't need any other distractions, as they were only a game and a half off the division lead.

Mark found his old home run form in the month of September, whacking 9 dingers in a month's time. With 5 games left to play, Mark was at 49, and many fans and reporters were pulling for him to reach the half-century mark. Coincidentally, Mark's wife, Kathy (who he had met when she was working as a ball girl for the USC team), was due in late September with their first child. With 2 games left, Kathy went into labor. Mark knew that his fans wanted him to reach 50, but to him it was an easy decision. He called Manager Tony La Russa and told him that he couldn't be with the team for the final two games. He needed to be at his wife's side.

Mark caught the first flight back to California and arrived at the hospital less than an hour before his child was born. To Mark, his newborn son, Matthew, was his 50th home run.

Mark was rewarded for his baseball efforts by being unanimously named American League Rookie of the Year. He also was sixth in the voting for the league's Most Valuable Player.

The A's were disappointed that they didn't make the playoffs, finally finishing third in the American League West division. They were, however, very excited about the talent that they had assembled on their ballclub. Everyone felt something special about this team, that they had the makings of a baseball dynasty. The following year would be a very exciting and interesting year, indeed.

• 5 •

ATHLETIC DYNASTY

The ingredients for a winning Athletics team were put in place during Mark's rookie year. Just a few adjustments to team chemistry were certain to create a winning formula, and as the 1988 baseball season got underway, many sportswriters were predicting that, led by the Bash Brothers, the Oakland A's would be vying for the division title.

Mark knew that the outrageous success of the previous season would be very difficult to match, and that he would have to endure constant comparison by reporters, fans, and even his friends. He therefore dedicated himself to a rigorous weight-training regimen in preparation for the following season. The *San Francisco Chronicle* reported: "Besides time in the weight room, McGwire is counting on a program of dietary supplements to help him keep his strength during the year. The top of his locker resembles a health-food store with jars of vitamins, amino acids, and something called 'Sudden Impact.'" This diet supplemented and reinforced a complete workout program. When Mark showed up for his second year in the majors, he was huge.

As the season began, the A's began playing terrific baseball, jumping to an early lead in the American League West division. While Mark was stroking the ball well enough, he was not popping them out of the ballpark like he had the previous year. The expectations from last season were getting the best of him. His batting average was hovering in the .250 range. Nonetheless, baseball fans elected Mark McGwire to start the 1988 All-Star Game—quite a feat for a second-year ballplayer!

While at the All-Star Game, many reporters asked Mark about his second year in the majors. Occasionally, Mac would become upset at these comparisons. "People say they don't expect me to hit 49 home runs again, but they do," Mark told one reporter. "I know people will always look at me differently because of that. They expect me to have 33 homers at the All-Star break. Give me a break." He added, "I'm tired of people comparing this year with last year. Every baseball person I talk to would like to have 19 home runs and 62 RBIs [his stats as of August, 1988]."

But most of the time Mark was thrilled, especially beacause his ball club was playing so well, safely positioned atop the division standings. If things continued as they were going, the A's would have no problem making the playoffs, with or without Mac's mammoth home runs.

In the final month of the 1988 season, Mark returned to his home run pace of the previous year, hitting a total of 13 dingers in

September. Mark's final statistics for the year were impressive: 33 homers (third highest in the league) and 99 RBIs. This was accomplished despite missing a week's worth of games toward the end of the season because of a sore back. It didn't bother Mark much, as he was excited to be making the playoffs in only his second season—the A's had won their division.

The American League Championship Series saw the A's pitted against the Boston Red Sox, and Mac was fired up, hitting .333 for the series. The A's made easy work of the Red Sox, sweeping the series in four straight games and earning the crown of AL Champs. They were going to the World Series.

Oakland's foes for the 1988 World Series were the Los Angeles Dodgers. Many reporters covering the fall classic thought that the Oakland power would be too much for the Dodgers, predicting a rather easy win for the A's. It didn't help matters much for the L.A. fans that their best hitter, Kirk

Gibson, was nursing an extremely sore hamstring and was unlikely to play.

In fact, Gibson did not play in the first game until the bottom of the ninth. With the Dodgers down by one run and a runner on base, Dodger manager Tommy Lasorda summoned the injured star from the locker room with two outs. Lasorda felt that if anyone would be able to conjure up some magic, it would be Kirk Gibson. And he was right. Gibson's ensuing home run is thought by many to be the most exciting play in recent baseball history. It set the tone for the rest of the series, as the A's lost the World Championship to the Dodgers in five games.

While Mark's teammates were disappointed with the loss, they knew that the better team had lost. They also realized that the winning formula that took them that far would still be around for the 1989 season, and they were eager for another opportunity to get back to the World Series.

* * *

Mark started the following season with a home run on opening day. Unfortunately, soon after, he was placed on the disabled list with a herniated disc. Mac missed only 14 games, but it took him out of his groove. Actually, Mark's home run stroke was still intact; it was his batting average that suffered. Much of the season, Mac was stuck in a hitting slump, and his average hovered around in a dismal range of .240.

Nonetheless, the A's were awesome that year, as many had projected them to be. Unfortunately for Oakland, the second-best team in the majors that season just happened to be in the same division—the Kansas City Royals. The Royals did their best to stay close, but as the season wound down, the power-hitting duo of McGwire and Canseco, combined with incredible pitching, simply proved to be too much. Mark had another strong year, hitting 33 homers (ranking third in the American League) and 94 RBIs. He was on fire during the AL Championship Series, hitting

.389 as the A's defeated the Toronto Blue Jays, winning four of five games.

Across the bay, the San Francisco Giants were also playing some impressive baseball, largely on the shoulders of Mac's old Olympic teammate and rival, Will Clark. It was poetic that these two teams would meet in the World Series that year, called by many "the Bay Area Series."

The A's World Series experience from the previous year was visible, as they used it to win the first two games of the series in Oakland. Mark played well, getting three hits in the opener and one in the second game. As the series shifted to San Francisco for game three, the A's were feeling confident. As the two teams warmed up before the game, a sizable earthquake rocked Candlestick Park (where the game was being held), and game 3 had to be postponed in order to repair structural damages.

A full 10 days later, the two teams finally reunited to continue the series. Oakland was definitely ready. Sweeping the series in four games, the players became World Champs. Unfortunately, what is most remembered for this series is not the champion team, but the devastating earthquake that many had watched on national television.

The following season, Mark was rewarded by the A's organization with a fat, one-year contract of $1.5 million. Some thought that Oakland's front office was attempting to inspire Mark's play. While they were thrilled with his home run and RBI output, his batting average was less than stellar. More importantly, there were whispers that Mark didn't appear to be as happy as a World Champ should be. Friends and fans were wondering if the pressure of being Mark McGwire was taking the fun out of the game for him.

In the 1990 baseball season, Mark became the first player in history to slug 30-plus homers in each of his first four full seasons. He also led the Athletics with 108 runs batted in that season as well as 156 games played. Getting elected to start his third consecutive All-Star Game was a nice recognition by his fans, but it did not mask Mark's deeper disappointment in his batting average. He was still struggling to hit over .250, which he felt was below his ability. Of course, most ballplayers would be pleased with his numbers, but Mark knew he could do better.

As the season progressed, talk of an Oakland dynasty was heard across the country, and the defending champs didn't miss a beat from their previous years of dominance. Winning the third-consecutive division title was almost commonplace, as was the four-game sweep of the Boston Red Sox. Three consecutive American League pennants is quite a feat, but the A's weren't as excited as one might expect. There was a strong sense among the team's players that they belonged in the pennant race. This diminished any element of surprise and perhaps a deeper sense of accomplishment.

Virtually everybody predicted an Oakland

sweep of the 1990 World Series against a young and hungry Cincinnati Reds team. Perhaps it was the overconfidence, or maybe they were simply outmatched by a more desirous Cincy team, but the series was a blowout. Unfortunately for Mark and his teammates, this time it was they who were on the losing side of a four-game sweep.

Over the previous three seasons, the A's had won over 300 games, won three division titles, and played in three separate World Series. Sadly for the Oakland fans, they had only one World Champion banner flying in Alameda Coliseum. Mark was eager for the off-season, hoping to find the cure for his sinking batting average.

Not only would the cure be elusive, but deeper problems were on the horizon.

SLUMPS AND INJURIES

The following season was not one that Mark McGwire recalls fondly. In 1991 Mark's baseball career sunk to rock bottom. With only 22 home runs, he ended his 4-year streak of 30-plus home run seasons. Even worse, his .201 average was a career low. It was an extremely difficult year for Mac, as he knew that he was capable of playing a much higher level of ball.

Living in the public eye, Mark felt scorn from hard-core A's fans. Even children who lived in his neighborhood were giving the big fella the business. One of Mark's friends told a *Sports Illustrated* reporter about this strange scenario.

"On a hill overlooking the pool [at Mc-Gwire's home] is this fence for the Alamo Elementary School. Well, kids would come to the fence at recess and yell, 'McGwire, you suck! McGwire, you stink!' It's got to hurt to have little kids yelling at you."

"How bad did it get?" Mark would later comment. "Well, for the first time, I disliked baseball. It was frustrating answering the question, over and over, 'Are you going to hit .200?' It was frustrating trying to climb out of a hole that got deeper and deeper. It was frustrating listening to all the hooting and hollering. I started joking in the clubhouse that I was going to give up baseball to shoot pool for a living, or maybe, like some of my friends, become a policeman. I was joking, but there was an element of truth in what I was saying."

Former teammate Dennis Eckersley commented about Mark's dark time. "He was going through hell, but he didn't wear it on his sleeve. All in all, he handled himself pretty well. In fact, he should be damn proud of the way he acted last year. For instance, sometimes a guy will let his hitting affect his fielding, but he had a great year at first base."

After the 1991 season ended, Mark spent a lot of time with friends outside of the baseball community. He went to a lot of comedy clubs and got to know many of the performing comedians. He played a lot of golf and hung out with PGA-tour player and friend Billy Andrade. Mark even caddied for him in an Australian tournament. About this experience Mac would say, "It was nice to get out in public and not be reminded about my season."

At the same time, Mark was increasing his weight-training program, adding 25 pounds of muscle to his previous 215-pound frame. "Beyond the physical benefits of working out," says McGwire, "weight training just makes you feel better about yourself." Mark also spent a lot of time with the A's new batting instructor, Doug Radar, who offered a very basic philosophy to hitting.

The simplification seemed to resonate well with Mac, as he was clearly guilty of thinking much too much about his hitting mechanics. When the 1992 season rolled around, Mark was eager to reclaim his reputation as an all-around batsman, not just a one-trick power hitter.

There was another major component to Mark's improvement that he felt necessary to address—his mental health. It wasn't as if Mark was losing his mind; it was just that he wasn't that happy. Part of this was that he was coming off a divorce from his former wife, Kathy, so he decided to see a therapist. He would later admit that while the therapy started as a "personal thing," before long it encompassed "everything." "Dealing with the media, dealing with fans, dealing with life. I got my mind straight, and everything followed." It was the first time in his life that he learned to appreciate the power of his own mind, and how he could apply this to the game of baseball.

Mark showed up to spring training in

1992 with a new look—longer hair and a new goatee. His extra muscles impressed a few teammates, and his happy disposition seemed to indicate to his coaches that he was ready to get back to playing solid baseball. As the season started, Mac showed his improvement, hitting 10 home runs in the month of April. He followed that with 8 homers in the month of May. Mark McGwire was back.

By season's end, Mark had put together a laundry list of accomplishments and awards. His ratio of a home run in every 11.1 plate appearances was a major league best. His total of 42 home runs was second in the league, and he had the highest slugging percentage at .585. Mark was fourth in AL Most Valuable Player voting and was selected by one news agency as Comeback Player of the Year.

Part of the magic of that season for Mark was that he accepted and embraced the fact that he was a home run hitter. Previously, he had been too caught up with the notion of being a complete hitter. But by acknowledging his home run prowess, it became fun again, and his 42 dingers put him in the company of baseball legends who reached a total of 200 homers in such a short time. Ironically, by accepting his home run strengths, Mark became more relaxed at the plate, and his overall batting average improved an amazing 67 points to .268.

While the A's weren't as dominant as they had been in previous years, they still managed to win the AL West division. They faced the Toronto Blue Jays in the League Championships, only this time as underdogs. Much like the rest of his teammates, Mark did not have a stellar series against the Blue Jays, getting only 2 hits in 19 at bats. As many expected, the A's were bounced from the playoffs by an eager Toronto ball club, who won the series in six games. Winning the series would have been a nice compliment to Mark's comeback, but he was just happy to be enjoying baseball again.

* * *

The next two seasons were perhaps the most frustrating for Mark McGwire. The 1993 season saw Mark play in only 27 games, primarily due to an injured left heel, for which he finally underwent surgery that September. Mac started the season on a roll, with 28 hits (15 for extra bases) and 24 RBIs in his first 25 games. However, he then missed the next 100 games after being placed on the disabled list on May 14.

Mark came into the 1994 season extremely eager to get back on the baseball diamond again. He had worked hard in the off-season to rehabilitate his heel. Sadly, it didn't take long for Mac to reinjure the same troublesome foot. While he was able to play in 47 games over the course of the season, his absence left a large void in the Oakland lineup. The lack of power and fielding expertise did not help the A's, as their good fortunes of the previous four years had finally ended.

No one was more frustrated with these

Mac Attack! Mark McGwire, home run king, hits another homer at Busch Stadium in St. Louis.
(AP/Wide World Photos)

Inset: A young Mark McGwire playing for the Oakland A's in 1987. *(UPI/Corbis-Bettmann)*

Mark hits the first grand slam of his major league career on August 12, 1988, against the California Angels. *(AP/Wide World Photos)*

Los Angeles Dodger Charles Johnson couldn't stop Big Mac from scoring the winning run in the ninth inning on July 19, 1998. *(AP/Wide World Photos)*

Practicing before the game against the Florida Marlins on September 3, 1998. Mac went on to hit two home runs that night, setting the National League record for home runs in a season. *(AP/Wide World Photos)*

The closer McGwire got to breaking the single-season home run record, the greater the media interest became. *(AP/Wide World Photos)*

Sammy Sosa and Mark McGwire laugh together during a news conference on September 7, 1998, discussing McGwire's 60 homers and Sosa's 58. *(AP/Wide World Photos)*

Mark appreciates Sammy's relaxed outlook on the game. Later that night, August 19, 1998, Mark hit #48 and #49 to win the game in extra innings.
(Agence France Presse/Corbis-Bettmann)

Mark signs autographs before a game—McGwire mania in full effect.
(AP/Wide World Photos)

Big Mac hitting his 61st home run, tying Roger Maris's major league single-season home run record. *(AP/Wide World Photos)*

Going, going, gone! Mark reacting to his 61st. *(AP/Wide World Photos)*

Mark enters the history books hitting his record-breaking 62nd home run.
(AP/Wide World Photos)

After an exciting trip around the bases, Mark comes home and celebrates his 62nd by lifting his son, Matthew, into the air.
(AP/Wide World Photos)

Mark and Sammy set a
record for class with
their open display of
mutual respect and
admiration.
(AP/Wide World Photos)

Showing respect for the
late Roger Maris, Mark
shares the moment with
the sons and daughter of
the former home run
king.
(AP/Wide World Photos)

injuries than Mark. Commenting on his bad heel, he said, "I thought it was fixed before. I'm sick and tired of being at 50 percent, 60 percent. I want to be well. That's the most irritating thing about this. It comes down to how I feel about my foot and how I feel about my career."

Mark was faced with a tough decision regarding the best form of treatment for his heel. He was afraid that another operation on his injured heel would technically fix the stress fracture but leave his foot weaker overall and thus more vulnerable for further injury. Eventually he decided to go for the surgery.

As the 1994 season progressed, labor problems between the players' union and the owners came to a peak. Eventually, a labor strike ensued, and the rest of the baseball season was cancelled. Mark was vocal about his union's rights, and some owners didn't take kindly to any ballplayer that was actively involved. The Oakland front office was no exception, and while the labor dispute was finally resolved for 1995, there was still a lot of ill will in baseball. Fans were disappointed, players were upset, and owners were holding grudges. The relationship between the Oakland front office and Mark McGwire was starting to get a little rocky. This was the start of the differences that would change Mark's career, as well as baseball history.

· 7 ·

REACHING 50

The 1994 season was a dark time for Mark McGwire. Not only was he injured for the second consecutive season—amidst an impressive comeback bid—but also there was a dark storm hanging over the institution of baseball. Labor problems between the players' union and the owners continued to fester. Every fan's worst nightmare was coming true. The Major League Baseball season would end as the players went on strike.

The strike caused significant damage in a number of ways. Players and owners were very stubborn in their unwillingness to bend regarding issues that appeared, to most fans, to be relatively insignificant, particularly in light of the fact that both players and owners were among the wealthiest segments of society. Most of the country saw both sides of the disagreement as extremely greedy, and the ill will generated by the strike would cast a dark shadow for some time. The players went on strike in August of 1994, the postseason was cancelled, and the work stoppage continued into the start of the 1995 season.

During this time, Mark expressed his feelings about players' rights. "You have a group of owners that wants to take away every right we've earned," he commented. "It seems like the owners want total control of everything." Not exactly words of negotiation, which was surprising to many, as Mark had always showed respect for the Haas family (owners of the Oakland Athletics), with whom he had always enjoyed a strong relationship. The fact that his comments were coming on the heels of two years of nonproduction (due to injury), did not make matters better.

As the early part of the 1995 season was cancelled because of the strike, fans started losing interest in the game of baseball. It got so bad that the owners and players agreed that if they didn't settle on some differences soon and get back out on the field, the institution of baseball might not survive. So without any real progress in labor relations, the owners and the players' organization agreed to set aside any differences, and resume a strike-shortened season as soon as possible. But the fans were still upset by each side's apparent greed and protested by not going to games. Attendance for the 1995 season was as low as anyone could recall. The strike was a failure in terms of bringing any sort of reform to labor relations, and the owners, fans, and players were equally frustrated.

When play finally resumed in May of 1995, Mark had a lot on his mind. He was frustrated with the strike, he was angry with his past two injury-filled seasons, and he was on the verge of renegotiating his contract with the A's organization. Somehow, Mac channeled all of this energy into positive output at the plate. In fact, despite the shortened season, Mark had as strong a season, statistically, as any other to date.

Mark hit 39 home runs in only 317 at bats—his sixth 30-plus HR season—with an unbelievable average of 1 home run in only 8.1 at bats. This home run ratio set a major league record, besting Babe Ruth's previous mark of 1 HR in 8.5 plate appearances. He also bested his own club slugging-percentage record by a whopping 67 points.

Mark's successful season put him squarely atop the list of statistical leaders in the history the Athletics organization. By the end of the season, Mac ranked first on the career chart for home runs and slugging percentage, third in total RBIs and extra-base hits, and fourth in on-base percentage, total bases, and walks. Mac had been an

Oakland A for his whole career, but his relationship with the front office was tenuous, at best.

Meanwhile, the Haas family was seriously considering bids from others who were interested in purchasing the Athletics organization. As the 1995 season progressed, it became increasingly clear that there would be new owners for the following season. Combined with a disappointing fourth-place finish, Mark knew there were soon to be changes in Oakland. And he was vocal about his interest in playing again for a winning team. While he didn't ask to be traded outright, he did say, "I don't want to be on a loser. I'm tired of losing."

The new A's owner, Steve Schott, heard these comments and shopped Mark's services around the league. Mark's name came up in a couple of potential deals that would have sent him to San Diego or possibly Cleveland. But when all was said and done, the A's realized that it was unlikely that they would receive comparable talent for Mark, so they wisely decided to hold on to Mac, at least for the time being. Responding to this latent vote of confidence, Mark entered the 1996 season wanting to prove himself once again.

As the A's prepared during spring training, there was a lot of hope for a successful season. There was a new owner, a new manager, Art Howe, and a core group of talented ballplayers. Mark had maintained his off-season training regimen and was in terrific shape entering spring training.

Two weeks into the camp, Mark was rounding the bases during an exhibition game when he heard a loud pop. It was his heel again, only this time it was his right foot. He couldn't believe it. He truly believed that his injuries were behind him, but unfortunately they were back again. Reporters that were covering training camp started asking about retirement, which Mark dismissed automatically. However, in the back of the minds of many involved with the A's organization, retirement was a very real possibility. Mark would not accept that and worked extra hard to get back in playing form. By the time his foot had healed, it was only late April, and he had only missed 18 games. This dramatic comeback energized Mark, and his performance at the plate reflected his newfound enthusiasm.

1996 was a banner year for Mark McGwire. In fact, it was statistically as good as his rookie year, 1987. Not only did he reach 50 home runs in 390 at bats (bettering Babe Ruth's old mark by 48 at bats), Big Mac's 52 home runs lead the majors. He also tied his own record of hitting a home run in every 8.13 at bats, and most impressively, Mark enjoyed his best batting average ever of .312, 60 points better than his career average. This was all accomplished despite missing the first three weeks of the season. Mark was rewarded for his abilities with his eighth selection to the AL All-Star Team in 10 seasons.

Breaking the 50-home-run mark was special. It was a plateau accomplished by very few players in the history of the game. When Mark hit his 50th, he was extremely proud, and he knew the first thing to do after the game—call his son Matthew. "He wasn't home," McGwire would tell a reporter after the game. "He was on the golf course."

The 50 home runs reinvigorated talk of the single season record of 61 home runs held by Roger Maris. When asked about this, Mark remained reflective, offering, "Someday somebody is going to break the home run record, and it will be an unbelievable feat. I don't sit here thinking about it because I realize how difficult it is. I mean, hitting a home run is probably the most difficult thing in sports, and doing it consistently in the second half of a season when teams aren't pitching to you is mind boggling." Most people agreed with this sentiment and knew that it would take an amazing individual to break the record.

As the 1997 season approached, once again trade rumors surfaced. Mark would be heading into the final year of his contract, and with the numbers he was recently putting up, he would command a huge salary. The A's were not sure that they wanted to invest so much money in a player who was entering his mid-30s, someone whose career had possibly already peaked. The A's cautiously decided to trade Mark, but because he had played 10 years, and more than five with the same club, he had to approve the deal.

Not sure where he would finish the season, Mark started off on fire. By the time the All-Star Game rolled around, he had amassed 31 total dingers. Once again he was selected to play in the All-Star Game, and once again his home run pace had captivated the imagination of the fans. Bad feelings from the players' strike still lingered, and overall baseball attendance was down. But fans were excited by Mac's shots, and pretty soon fans started coming out before the game, just to watch Mark's batting practice, which was always an impressive exhibition of power hitting.

After the All-Star Game, it became more

certain that Mark would be traded. And as more reporters started inquiring about which his next team might be, Mark became distracted, hitting only 3 more home runs in the month of July. Everyone acknowledged that he was off the pace to break the home run record. Sportswriters wrote that any talk of breaking Maris's record was silly. It was a record for the ages.

The deadline for trading a player who can still be eligible for the playoffs is July 31. Up to then, only two teams were making serious inquiries—Toronto and St. Louis. Because staying close to his son was his top priority, Mac eventually approved his trade to the Cardinals. Mark was overwhelmed by the reception of the St. Louis fans. He responded to the new-found love by hitting 24 homers in the last two months, finishing the season with 58 total home runs, the most hit in a single season since Roger Maris. Because he had fallen so far off the pace while the trade rumors were circling in July, there was less talk about the home run chase. But as the season's end drew near, the country was watching. His head-to-head battle with Seattle superstar Ken Griffey, Jr. was a terrific story that held the country's attention. While neither broke the record, baseball was suddenly fun again, and people started to believe that the most revered record in all of sports was being toyed with.

Mark loved the St. Louis fans, and the ball club loved him. In late September 1997, Mark chose not to test the free-agent waters and signed a three-year, $30-million deal with the Cardinals. At the press conference, a teary McGwire announced that $1 million of his annual salary would go to charities to aid abused children.

The St. Louis fans and owners knew that they had someone very special, and Mark knew that. He also knew that things were starting to come together for something phenomenal to happen. Mark was happy with his life, his ball club, and with his playing ability. 1998 would be a very special year. Little did he know how special it would be.

· 8 ·

HOME RUN FEVER

Soon after the 1997 season, Mark began receiving a tremendous amount of media attention. Many reporters were curious about Mark's sudden improvement, not just at the plate, but in his overall attitude. "I'm grounded now," he told a reporter. His son, Matthew, played a large part in his outlook—that and his positive relationship with his ex-wife Kathy and her new husband, of whom he said, "He's a great guy." But it was his son, Matthew, who continued to be his source of inspiration. Regarding an earlier visit from his son, Mark said, "He brought a buddy. It was just the three of us the whole weekend. I had the greatest time in the world." Mark's overall happiness translated to confidence at the plate, baseballs in the bleachers, and joy amongst the legions of loyal St. Louis fans.

On the opening day of the 1998 season, Mark and his Cardinals were playing host to the Los Angeles Dodgers. With two outs and the bases loaded in a scoreless game, and the crowd going wild on opening day, McGwire launched a blast into the left-field seats in the fifth inning. With that game-winning shot, Mark became the first Cardinal to hit an opening-day grand slam. He also set the tone for what would be a phenomenal year.

The Cardinals' spring began with plenty of anticipation about Mark McGwire and how many home runs he could hit in his first full season in St. Louis. The way that Mark was swinging the bat in the month of April only brought more excitement, attention, and focus. All around the city of St. Louis, fans would stop whatever they were doing when Mark came to the plate. Questions about what the Cardinals did on any day were followed quickly by a question about whether Mark hit any out of the park and how far they went.

There were plenty of home runs to talk about: the opening-day grand slam, the 12th-inning game-winner in Game 2, the 3 home runs in one game on April 14. But Mark was helping the Cardinals in ways other than home runs. Not only was he offering solid defensive play at first base, but by the end of April he was also hitting .318 with 36 RBIs and had been walked a league-leading 27 times. (Opposing pitchers avoided giving Big Mac any decent pitches to pounce on.) Needless to say, Mark was extremely pleased with his own performance. The Cardinals were not doing as well. Problems with pitching and all-around inconsistency would keep the Cards below .500. But it was early in the season, and with a few adjustments, this team could be a force.

As the year moved into the month of May, Mark continued his torrid pace. In fact, in many ways it was as big a month for Mark as the previous month had been. On May 16, batting against the Marlins' starter (and World Series MVP) Livan Hernandez, Mark hit a 545-foot home run. By denting a sign (which later received a big Band-Aid) above the batter's screen in center field and almost landing in the luxury boxes, the 545-foot home run was the longest ever at Busch Stadium.

On May 19, playing at Philadelphia's Veterans Stadium, Mac had yet another amazing day at the plate, hitting 3 home runs in one game. By doing so, Mark became just the 12th player in big-league history to have two 3-homer games in the same season. Also in the month of May, Mark hit his 400th career home run, reaching this milestone faster than anyone in baseball history. Simply put, Mark's red-hot start in April only improved into May. In one seven-day span, Mark hit 8 home runs, a phenomenal feat to be sure.

Coming into the season, baseball fans were keeping a close eye on Mark's awesome power. But after the April and May that he had enjoyed, it seemed that everyone with even the slightest interest in baseball was paying close attention. People that had forsaken the sport because of the strike three years earlier were scanning the sports pages, looking for Mac's results or pouring into the stands to see Mac go to work. The McGwire phenomenon grew to the point that an opposing manager would intentionally walk him with the bases empty in an extra-inning game just so he couldn't hit a home run. On Memorial Day, ESPN cut to the Cardinals game every time McGwire came to the plate. It was only May, but the whole world seemed to be watching.

Entering the month of June, the Cardinals had a tough time winning games, and while Mark continued to hit baseballs out the park, the home runs did not come in buckets as they did in April and May. That is to say, Big Mac didn't have any multi-homer games. He did, however, hit 10 homers (and 19 RBIs) to bring his total of round-tripppers up to 37 entering the month of July.

Mark's home run pace continued to captivate the imagination of baseball fans young and old, and the already intense nationwide attention only increased. With the team playing on the road for much of June, and the Cardinals' schedule entering the interleague portion, batting practice in other ballparks became a spectacle in its own right. Tens of thousands of fans would come to a ballpark roughly two hours before the start of the game, just to watch Big Mac take practice cuts. Of course, the real spectacle was the fact that it was not unusual for Mark to hit 10 to 15 of his 20 practice pitches over the outfield fence. Mark's display of pure power at the plate brought fans to their feet in anticipation.

Sometimes, however, batting practice, and the commotion it was causing, would be bit of an ordeal. Mark talked about not taking BP to reduce some of the media distractions. (The team finally issued some guidelines for interviews by out-of-town reporters.) After rules were set and fans were kept out of everyone's way, batting practice became enjoyable. Teams that were hosting the Cardinals would see their attendance figures shoot up when Mac came to town; sometimes more fans would arrive for Cardinal batting practice than had shown up for the previous game. Baseball was suddenly fun again.

In April and May, Mark McGwire had set himself apart from the rest of the league. The month of June would see two more ballplayers enter the home run derby. Ken Griffey, Jr. was no stranger to this territory, as he had battled Mac head-to-head the previous season. He was also no stranger to swatting baseballs over the outfield fence, as he finished the month of June with 33 dingers, just 4 off of Mark's pace. Seattle fans knew that Junior was just as capable of catching Maris's mark of 61 homers as anyone else. The home run excitement had spread from St. Louis to Seattle.

The other ballplayer to enter the world of home run dominance was Chicago Cubs outfielder Sammy Sosa. Sammy had not gotten off to a huge start in the first two months of the season, hitting a respectable, but not dominant, 12 home runs in April and May. Sammy's month of June, however, would be something for the ages.

Actually, going back to May 25, Sammy slammed 21 home runs in 22 games up to June. The single-month record for home runs was held by a little-known player by the name of Rudy York, who played for the Detroit Tigers in the 30s. In the first 21 days of June, Sosa had hit more homers (17) than any man had ever hit in that month. With nine days left, it seemed clear that York's record was in serious danger.

As Sammy approached this record, the media attention shifted from Mac to Sosa, simply because he was the hottest player in the country. As everyone expected, Sosa, who ended the month with 21 round-trippers, smashed the single-month record. He also entered July with 33 home runs, just 4 off of Mac's 37, and the same as Ken Griffey, Jr.

As the heart of the baseball season approached, the country was mesmerized by the number of baseballs flying off of the bats of Mac, Sammy, and Junior. Fortunately for Mark, this meant that there was less focus on just him. Sports reporters and journalists would have to split their time between Seattle, Chicago, and St. Louis. It was a much-needed reprieve from the sometimes-claustrophobic media, which was starting to get on his nerves.

As the homers racked up, some fans and reporters were certain that Maris's record wouldn't last through the end of the season. However, more columnists knew that every player goes through a tired phase in late July and August, and that 61 home runs in one season would be a very difficult target to hit. Nonetheless, the power display was starting to raise questions as to why this season was so conducive for home-run hitters. Was the ball juiced? Were the players juiced? Were the ranks of pitchers significantly thinned due to expansion? These questions were asked regularly on sports radio talk shows. A national debate had started.

· 9 ·

HISTORICAL PERSPECTIVE

Baseball has been a part of the American heritage for well over one hundred years. So interwoven is baseball into the rich tapestry of the American story, foreign dignitaries have returned to their home countries acknowledging that one could not understand the American sensibility without first understanding the nuances of the game of baseball. Throughout the growth and development of the United States, there has always been the constant of baseball, through the ups and downs, wars and depressions. Even as the nation's interest in the game has ebbed and flowed with good times and bad, baseball has remained true to its own spirit, as no other game offers the idiosyncrasies, personalities, and spectacle of this great sport.

Despite rivalries, most athletes agree that there is nothing more difficult in all of sports than hitting a home run. The physics alone of hitting a ball out of the park is baffling even to scientists who study such things. Considering that a batter has just a split second to track a 90-mile-an-hour fastball (thrown toward him from only 66 feet away), swing a two-pound piece of lumber around quickly enough to meet the ball, then drive it some 400 feet (between the foul poles and over the fence)—it's no wonder that the home run is also the most celebrated and exciting event in all of sports.

The players that have proven themselves adept at hitting home runs have always been among the most popular players in the league. Logically, the players that hold the home run records are typically viewed as being among the best to ever play the game.

Babe Ruth is generally viewed as the

greatest ballplayer of all time—in large part because of his tendency to put the baseball into the outfield bleachers. Playing for the New York Yankees throughout the 20s, the Babe held two of the most prestigious records in all of baseball for a very long time—the single-season and career marks for home runs.

In 1927, the Babe went yard 60 times—an outstanding feat by any measure. But what makes that mark so much more interesting is the fact that, other than his Yankee teammate Lou Gehrig (who hit 42 in the same season), only two other batters in the majors hit over 20 home runs that season. Talk about outdistancing the competition. After Ruth set the record, most felt that no one would come close. And it would take 35 years for another player to make a serious challenge—another Yankee, Roger Maris.

Because the Babe had been *the* Yankee icon, many New Yorkers were actually hoping that Roger Maris would not break the record in 1961, sometimes even openly cheering against him. As the season wound down, the media attention and the stress that came with trying to beat the Babe's record eventually got to Maris. So stressed was he, in fact, that large clumps of his hair were falling out of his head. About this time, Roger would recall, "During the last couple of weeks [of the season] I was half nuts, I had splitting headaches, I was smoking twice as much as I normally do, and the crowds, tension, the same questions over and over again, were driving me out of my mind." Maris was a straightforward gentleman who came from the simpler plains of North Dakota. He wanted to play as well as he could, but he clearly did not enjoy all of the scrutiny that came with his record chase.

When he finally broke Babe's record with his 61st home run, he felt pride in his achievement, as well as relief that all the attention had passed. But because the over-all length of the season had grown since 1927 from 154 to 162 games, the baseball commissioner announced that Maris's record would have an asterisk next to it. Many felt this to be a slap in the face of Maris and his tremendous year. It wasn't until his record withstood the test of time— holding up for over three decades—that Roger Maris would get the respect he deserved.

Since it would be such a long time until the home run chase of 1998 would occur, many writers, players, and fans compared the home run kings of each era. Was hitting 60 home runs in 1998 as impressive a feat as it had been in 1961 or 1927?

There is a general, albeit subjective, belief that since athletes are better today than in 1927, it must be harder to hit homers today. Baseball is unique among team sports in that we have a wealth of statistical data to work with, but even people who study this information in detail are unable to completely agree on how to compare statistical performance in baseball from one decade to the next.

Simply because home runs were rarer, raw statistical data would indicate that it has become far *easier* to hit homers today compared to 1927. That is to say, since there were fewer total home runs hit in 1927, it must have been more difficult then. But baseball is far too subtle for that basic comparison. The overall increase in home runs from season to season can likely be attributed to the exact same reasons why sports records in general continue to fall year after year. Athletes just continue to get stronger, faster, and bigger. Certainly today's pitchers are bigger and throw harder than their counterparts in the 20s but the best pitcher of the last decade has been a smallish control pitcher named Greg Maddux.

Throughout baseball history one can see cycles where hitting statistics have risen and then fallen in ways that are difficult to explain. League expansion, changes in ballparks, changes in the strike zone or height of the mound, possibly even in the compression of the ball itself—all have an effect on these statistics. This is what makes it so difficult to compare different periods of upward and downward trends in home run hitting.

When baseball historians of the next millennium look at the increased home runs of the 1990s, they will likely point to an expanded league and the diluted pitching talent. Simple math tells us that if there are 50 pitching stars playing for only 24 teams, batters will ultimately face better pitching more often than if the same talent is spread over 30 teams. In fact, 1961 was an expansion year, and home run totals rose dramatically over those of 1960. Roger Maris, who was the AL MVP in 1960 and thus not a one-year wonder, went from the low 40s in 1960 to his record 61.

It is interesting to note that after 1961, baseball officials seemed to make it harder to hit home runs, as the strike zone and mound height were incrementally altered. Hitting trended downward dramatically, and by the end of the 60s, players were hard-pressed to hit .300 and 30 home runs. After 1961, only Willie Mays in 1965 and George Foster in 1977 hit over 50 home runs until Cecil Fielder did it in 1990. By comparison, there will likely be nine players with 50-plus home run seasons since the 1994 strike. There have been only nineteen 50-plus HR seasons (by ten players) in the 75 years prior.

The excitement of the 1998 season—and the well-documented home run chase—brought renewed interest to baseball's rich heritage. The torrential downpour of base-balls into the bleachers in St. Louis, Chicago, and Seattle created its own media storm. Beyond the coverage of every game, at bat, and pitch thrown to Sammy, Junior, and Mac, sports programs were suddenly presenting segments on the history of home run records, the game of baseball, and the legends that preceded the current home run chase. Magazines and newspapers that nor-mally ignored sports coverage saw the home run chase as a great opportunity to sell copies, and they started tracking the pace. Just as Roger Maris had been troubled by the attention, a lot of fans predicted that the media would increasingly perturb Mark, Sammy, and Junior.

AUGUST SLUMP

Every year, one of the great traditions of baseball occurs just after the midway point of the season. The All-Star Game honors the best players in the league and embraces interleague rivalry—all in good fun. As has been the case in many professional All-Star experiences, the actual game is only a component of a much larger set of festivities. Only recently did Major League Baseball begin having pregame activities. Easily the most popular is the home run derby held the day before the All-Star Game.

Sort of a competitive batting practice, the home run derby is fairly simple. Each participant gets 10 swings, and the players who hit the most out of the park advance to the next round. The 1998 All-Star festivities (including this competition) would be held in a park that was extremely conducive to homers—Denver's Coors Field. While always a popular affair, the participation of Mark McGwire, Sammy Sosa, and Ken Griffey, Jr. ensured that there was a *lot* of hype surrounding the home run derby.

What was meant to be an exhibition of Mac's power ultimately turned into a display of Junior's consistency. After first announcing his intentions to skip the competition, Griffey, Jr. won the contest going away. Mac did not fare so well, hitting only four of the 10 pitches out of the park. Except for the towering, 510-foot shot that was the longest of the day, Mac looked more like a line-drive hitter than a home run king and was bounced after the first round.

Because so many were eager to see his power display, many thought that Mark simply crumbled under the pressure. In the postderby interview, Mac seemed annoyed with all of the hype. It was the first time that Mac looked like he wasn't having fun. The All-Star Game was another disappointment, with Big Mac going 0-for-2 with a walk. Everywhere he went, there was a reporter sticking a microphone in his face.

"I don't know if I'll ever enjoy the requests to talk about myself. That's just not me as a person. But I've come to realize that I have to do something about it, and I have to talk about it." When a reporter asked him a question about something other than home runs, Mac sat back and applauded in mock approval. What was meant to be funny appeared to be more of a display of annoyance. Was the pressure starting to get to Mac?

As the rest of the season got underway, it was clear that Mark was feeling the weight of the world's expectations upon his shoulders. He continued to put up strong numbers, but was enjoying himself a lot less. Mark was uncomfortable with the media scrutiny that came with the home run chase, not because of a lack of patience, but more because he was a genuinely modest and humble gentleman who simply didn't enjoy talking about himself so much. It had been reported that Mac's frustration with masses of reporters was due to his claustrophobia. The horde of reporters that were now covering his every move—on and off the field—was not exactly the best thing for someone who grew fidgety in close or cramped quarters.

Despite Mark's visible lack of patience—both at the plate and behind the microphone—July did have its own set of McGwire highlights, not least of which was Mark's smashing of Johnny Mize's Cardinal record for homers in a single season. It took Mark just 104 games in 1998 to hit his 44th home run and break Mize's record. But by the standards that Mark had set from the previous months, July was fairly quiet. He hit just 8 home runs and had some pretty long gaps between dingers. Though

McGwire always retained his lead, Ken Griffey Jr. and Sammy Sosa continued to move closer into the home run chase.

August began while Mark's home run pace slowed dramatically, and the press coverage increased. Mac was exasperated with the media "circus" that was following him, and three weeks into August, it looked as though his pursuit of Roger Maris's home run record was going to slowly fade away. To make matters more difficult, opposing pitchers were not throwing anything near the strike zone when Mark came to bat. In fact, most pitchers were downright terrified of McGwire.

"With McGwire, pitchers aren't comfortable looking in there at him," Cubs manager Jim Riggleman said. "They just don't feel good throwing it up there to him."

By mid-August, Mac had walked 121 times this season, just 30 short of the NL record of 151 walks by Barry Bonds in 1996. The Cubs alone had walked McGwire 16 times in their first seven games this year.

Fans and players alike were growing frustrated. "I never have problems with [putting a runner on base] late in the game," Cardinals manager Tony La Russa said. "That's baseball. But the first five or six innings? Never. It should be their best against your best."

This was helping neither Mark's slump nor his peace of mind. "What's getting to him is not getting pitches to hit," La Russa said. "That's the only thing stressing him."

Perhaps this was the case, as the Cards manager indicated. Maybe all Mark needed were a few good fastballs across the plate to help him break his home run drought. Maybe Mark had adjusted to the media scrutiny, and it was just a matter of getting good looks at the plate. Things took a turn for the worse, however, when an element of controversy entered the Mark McGwire story.

Amidst Mark's home run drought, it was reported that Mark McGwire had been using a testosterone-boosting compound for the previous year. While technically only a dietary supplement, critics were eager to call it a steroid and therefore discount Mac's accomplishments. Many were calling for an asterisk next to any home run record because Mark was taking "andro" (androstenedione) a pill that allows enhanced performance through the body's natural production of testosterone, before his weightlifting sessions. Never mind that the use of these pills is well within the rules of drug use defined by Major League Baseball.

Reporters were no longer comfortable asking Mark about the chase. In mid-August, people were beginning to accept the notion that Mark McGwire was just another mortal man, unable to rise above the distractions and hype of modern baseball. After some debate, most agreed that "andro" was quite different than anabolic steroids (which *are* illegal in all pro sports), and the controversy went away. But it was yet another distraction for Mark, and his performance at the plate did not go unaffected.

The numeric comparisons of Maris, McGwire, and Sosa were graphically displayed in virtually every daily sports page across the country. The controversy, media scrutiny, and lack of hittable pitches, combined with the late-summer heat, had an adverse effect on Mark's power production. In the first 18 days of the month of August, McGwire had hit just two home runs—falling behind the record-chasing pace for the first time. But that only set the scene for what would be one of the most amazing weeks of the entire season for McGwire.

· 11 ·

BACK ON PACE

As Mark McGwire saw fewer pitches to swing at, his home run total stagnated, and some of the hype surrounding the record chase subsided. Ken Griffey, Jr. was also in the middle of his own August home run slump, which is a common occurrence among power hitters.

But whereas Mac and Junior grew tired in the dog days of summer, Sammy Sosa was gaining speed and momentum—continuing to smash the ball all over Wrigley Field. Suddenly Sosa was on Mark's heels in the chase for 61. It was suddenly a two-man race to break the record, with the leader faltering and Sammy gaining ground. On

August 18, Sammy tied Mark McGwire by hitting his 47th home run.

In an unseemly turn of events, the day following Sammy's 47th and league-tying home run, the Cardinals traveled to Chicago's Wrigley Field for a matchup between two storied rivals. Sports reporters were declaring this a personal matchup between the two players, a battle to see who would earn the title of Home Run King. These two home run sluggers were chasing history, and the entire nation was paying attention.

Before the game even started, Mac and Sammy had a chance to hang out together before a well-attended batting practice. The two had a friendly conversation and discussed how each was holding up under the intense media scrutiny. After exchanging quick hugs, the two went back to their respective clubhouses, each with a much deeper appreciation for what they were going through. This interaction had a big impact on Mark's outlook on the media.

For the first time, Mark realized that there was someone else going through the same frustrating set of questions and hyper-analysis, and that he was not alone. Mark also noted Sammy's easygoing personality, the way in which Sosa was having fun with all of the attention, not letting it "get to" him. This would be a key discovery. Walking back to the clubhouse, Mark was energized. He was having fun again. He was ready to play.

Throughout the entire season, up to this point, Mark had lead Sammy in home runs. On August 19, for the first time all season, Sosa passed McGwire.

For about an hour.

Sammy took over the major-league home run lead at 48 with a fifth-inning drive off Cardinals starter Kent Bottenfield. But Mac, homerless in 20 previous at bats, tied Sosa—and the game—in the eighth. He then passed Sosa and won the game in the 10th with his 49th homer of the season, as the Cardinals overcame the Cubs, 8–6.

Cardinals manager Tony La Russa said, "What a thrill to be at the park as a fan or a teammate to see both those guys come through."

After falling off the pace, Mac caught Roger Maris with 49 homers in 124 games. Maris, on his way to 61 in 1961, had 49 after 124 games and 50 after 125. Mark was just a dinger away from 50, which would make him the first player in history to have three successive years of 50 or more home runs. Still, questions of an ongoing slump lingered.

One of the keys to amassing numerous home runs in a single season is the avoidance of prolonged periods of nonproduction. Keeping a positive outlook, remaining focused, avoiding injury, and stamina are all vital components to a record-breaking year. Outside of his midseason grouchiness and physical weariness in August, Mark McGwire had thus far successfully achieved these goals. For Mac to break Maris's record, he would have to return to his early season form and hope that his two-homer game against the Cubs would stem his late-summer slump.

Slump? What slump?

To keep things in proper perspective, one must realize that his slump is another batter's hot streak. Most big-league ballplayers hit a home run once in roughly every 34 at bats. By way of comparison, in 1998, Mark McGwire hit the ball out of the park once in an average of 7 or 8 plate appearances. If Mac goes 20 straight at bats without a dinger, the baseball community screams, "Slump!" Virtually any other big-league player would love to go yard once in every 20 chances.

So with two dramatic shots in Wrigley field, Mark was back on a pace to break 61. He was also one shot away from his 50th, a personal goal that he had set at the outset of the season.

Mark had said all along that the chase to the home run record really wasn't on until somebody got to 50. "That's when you guys are going to have to ask some really good questions because you've been wasting them the last six months," he said, jokingly. But about hitting number 50, Mark added, "It will mean a lot. It will be quite a feat."

After the game in Chicago, the Cardinals headed to Shea Stadium to face the New York Mets. The two home runs against the Cubs had people talking as if Mac was back. New York sportswriters are notoriously tough on professional athletes, and many of them were curious to see how Big Mac would react to a difficult media environment. As had been the case wherever Mark McGwire and the Cardinals showed up, the stadium was at capacity with fans hoping to see Mark's 50th homer.

In the seventh inning of the first game of a doubleheader, Mark lifted Willie Blair's fourth pitch an estimated 369 feet and over the left-field fence. Normally, Mark's particular about running around the bases without showing any emotion, but this time Mac displayed uncommon happiness on this home run trot, pumping his fist into the air twice around first base and clapping his hands exuberantly as he jogged around third. He punched the air again as he drew near the plate.

"I've seen him win a World Series game with a homer, and he wasn't even close to that," commented Card's manager Tony La Russa when asked about Mac's display of excitement. "That was the most emotional thing I've ever seen." Mac said what he felt on his home run trot was "relief. You get to 49 and you have one more. Sometimes it takes time to get that extra one."

As icing on the cake, he followed with a first-inning shot in the second game that would be his 51st home run, just inside the left-field foul pole. With these dramatic shots, Mark totaled 161 overall home runs, more than any before in a three-season span. He also became the first player ever to have three consecutive 50–home–run seasons. "It's history," Mac would comment. "I'm the first baseball player to do it for three consecutive years. Thousands of power hitters have played this game, and nobody has ever done it. I can sit here and say that I'm the first major-league player to ever do it. I'm pretty proud of it."

Mark would hit his 52nd and 53rd in consecutive games while playing in Pittsburgh, wrapping up a phenomenal span of 6 home runs in five days. He was back on pace to join Ruth and Maris as the only big leaguers to ever hit the 60-home-run mark.

Mark's slump was over. When asked what, if anything, had changed in his game, Mac replied, "I'm not as tired. I'm getting pitches to hit. It's a matter of centering the ball. And I got two balls to hit today. It's a tough thing to do when everybody wants it to be done. But Sammy hit 20 in June. You've got to get hot. If you get hot, it can be done."

Mark also spoke about the importance of a positive attitude and confidence. "You have to be confident in what you do, or this game of baseball will whip you in a heartbeat," McGwire said. "Once in a while, everybody gets down on themselves in the game of baseball, but you've got to stay positive."

The scrutiny in the last six weeks would only become more intense, and Mac was ready, becoming at peace with the press. "Every move we make, every swing we take, every home run we hit . . . he's in the lead, no, he's in the lead . . . it's going to be that way every day till the end of the season," he said. This positive outlook had to affect his game. Plus, he was swinging the bat well. Mark knew that if he could enter the month of September having hit 50 home runs, he would have a chance to make history.

All season, in fact, Mac had said that the time to start talking about breaking the record of 61 homers in one season would come if someone had hit 50-homers by September 1. Finally, with his 50th and 51st, America was talking. "I have to say I do have a shot," McGwire said. "But I know it's going to be tough."

· 12 ·

MARK'S FRIEND SAMMY

Mark McGwire's red-hot streak of 6 homers in a five-day span gave new attention to the record chase. Mac seemed to transfer this increased focus and energy into his own enthusiasm, which in turn motivated Sammy Sosa. The bottom line was this—Mac and Sammy were hitting baseballs out of the park, and the country was enjoying every day of this spectacle.

On August 26, the Cardinals were hosting the Florida Marlins. In the bottom of the eighth inning, nursing a 1–0 lead, Mac strode to the plate. Since it had been three days since he last went yard, the crowd came to their feet, anxiously awaiting what they hoped would be number 54. After getting a called strike on the first pitch, Marlin right-hander Justin Speier threw a 90-mile-an-hour fastball that never reached the catcher's mitt. Instead, Big Mac sent the ball soaring 509 feet to deep center, hitting high off the green hitter's background behind center field of Busch Stadium. The crowd gave their approval with a thunderous ovation when Mac crossed home and touched fists with the Cardinal batboy, his 10-year-old son, Matt.

The following Saturday, while the Cards were hosting the Atlanta Braves, Mark McGwire came to the plate for his first at bat. After being declared out on a called third strike, Mark argued vehemently with the home plate umpire. After giving him three warnings for arguing, rookie ump Sam Holbrook kicked Mark out of the game—a game that was eventually won by the Atlanta Braves, 4–3.

Holbrook, who joined the National League as a full-time umpire in the spring, ejected Cardinals manager Tony La Russa first, then Mark, and then pitching coach Dave Duncan, who had complained from the dugout. The fans, who had been hoping to see a McGwire home run, were extremely disappointed in Mac's ejection, and sometimes threw baseballs onto the field to express their disapproval.

The emotional outburst was unusual for Mark, a player who takes pride in his on-the-field behavior. Once again the question was asked: Was the pressure getting to him? "I don't know why we're making such a big deal out of it," McGwire said. "It happens every day. Heat of the moment. It's done with. It's over."

The next day was the last game of a week-long home stand against the Braves. Even though the outcome of the game would have little impact on postseason play, there was a sense of electricity to this game reminiscent of a pennant race. Of course, the capacity crowd—joined by a national audience viewing the game on *Sunday Night Baseball* on

ESPN—were watching the Great Home Run Race. This was made even more interesting by events that had taken place earlier that day. It seems that Junior would hit his 47th and Sammy would hit his 54th, tying the current total of the St. Louis star.

While everyone had tuned in to see Mac hit one out, no one expected the drama that came with his bottom-of-the-seventh, three-run shot that gave the Cardinals an 8–7 victory over the Braves. The home run came off of veteran reliever Dennis Martinez, and ended up an estimated 501 feet from home plate. Mac's shot would tie the National League record held by Hack Wilson. When told of this, Mac replied, "I didn't even know that was the record. In spring training, it was one of my goals to get [50 homers]. Now, everything is basically icing on the cake as far as what I can do to strive for, I guess, what America wants." He then added, "Sometimes I surprise myself. It's unbelievable. But I'll tell you what, I'll give it my best shot."

Two days later, Mark and his Cardinal

team would be playing in Florida. With the Cards up 4–0, and former World Series MVP Livan Hernandez on the mound, Mark sent a seventh-inning fastball deep to the center field seats. It's almost unheard of for a visiting player to be called out of the dugout by applause, but this season and this player were different.

Later in the same game, in the top of the ninth inning, Mark sent the first pitch he received approximately 472 feet to the center field seats. Mark would take his second curtain call of the night, and later say about this magic evening, "Let's just ride the wave and see what happens."

With 10 home runs in the last 12 days, Mark McGwire was the toast of the nation. News programs would lead their evening shows with an update of Mac's latest feat. Newspaper columns urging Mark on were appearing across the nation, and it seemed like wherever one went, there was no escaping the youthful and enthusiastic discussion of the home run race.

Th[...] phenomen[...]g day, Mark had another Cards up 7–0, [...] at the plate. With the upper deck of Mi[...]ook a 2–1 pitch to the for number 58, tying hi[...] Pro Player Stadium the previous season. It woul[...] rsonal record set more inning for Mac t[...] only take one record, hitting home run number 59 to left-center field. Only Roger Maris and Babe Ruth have hit more home runs in a season, and Mark was called out for his second curtain call of that night, his fourth in two days—all at an opposing team's stadium!

The ongoing race between Mark and Sammy was brewing as well. Even though Mac had hit a preposterous 12 home runs over a two-week span, Slammin' Sammy was staying right with him, having hit 13 of his own homers in the month of August. Sosa's hot streak coincided with Mark's early-August slump, so that in early September Mark held only a 2–home run lead over his Chicago competitor.

With the media coverage now peaking at

a fever pitch, many repo.s ...re eager to bitter rivals. portray Mark and Sastion was tossed But every time ach would reply with toward either pla the utmost resp for the other.

When ask. directly about Sosa, Mark said, "I'm extremely happy for Sammy. Sammy is having a magical year. A way better year than I'm having. His team is right there in the wild-card race, he's driven in quite a few more runs than I have, he's hit for a higher average. Tip your hat to him."

After Sosa learned that Mark had been ejected from the game against the Braves, Sammy reacted sadly, then called over some Chicago sportswriters and asked them to print a quote, hoping that Mark would see it. "Mark, please don't do that again. Get your four or five at bats. I'm pulling for you." When asked about the controversy over Mark's use of the androstenedione supplement, Sosa frowned. "Don't pick at Mark," he said. "Let Mark be Mark, and let me be me. Let us have fun."

When hearing of this, Mac laughed. "Sammy always says 'I'm The Man.' But he's The Man, too."

It was clear that these two gentlemen had fostered a deep understanding of each other. Living under a media microscope had been difficult, particularly for Mark. Sammy showed Mac how to enjoy the process. Likewise, every time Mac was asked about Sammy, he was quick to point out what a tremendous year Sosa was enjoying—all-around statistically better than his own. The mutual respect and class that these two players were displaying for each other was almost as amazing as the 500-foot shots they were sending out of stadiums.

On Saturday, September 5, the Cardinals hosted to the Cincinnati Reds. Nursing a lead of only 2 homers over Slammin' Sammy Sosa, Big Mac came out in the first inning and crushed a 2–0 pitch into the left-field bleachers of Busch Stadium, giving him 60 total round-trippers for the season, more than anyone has hit since Roger Maris hit 60 in 1961. No longer was there a question of Mac's ability to break the record. The new question was *when* he would hit 61 and 62. Even more important to fans and baseball historians alike, *could* Mark McGwire stave off the furious pace of his friend Sammy Sosa?

Mac's 60th dinger gave him a little breathing room in the race—three more than Sammy's 57. But that wouldn't last for long. Shortly thereafter, Sosa hit his 58th while playing at Pittsburgh. These two ball players were incredible! Mac hit a home run to increase his lead and within hours Sosa answered. Two days later, the competition would move to one stadium—the Cardinals were hosting the Cubs. The world was watching, eager to see history made.

Before the first game of the series, Sammy and Mark held a press conference to discuss the 118 home runs the two had hit thus far in the season. While each player had gone out of his way to complement the other in previous quotes, this was the first time that they would appear together. They entered the room laughing, clearly comfortable with the environment, and enjoying each other's company. "Like I've been saying, your heart's not beating if you're not excited about today," said Mac about the day's game.

When a reporter, possibly trying to create a rift between two, asked the two of them who was The Man, both paused to think about it. Then Sammy interrupted the silence by saying, "He is The Man in the United States; I am The Man in the Dominican Republic."

Mark laughed and agreed. For although these two ballplayers came from particularly different backgrounds—Sammy grew up in the economically depressed streets of the Dominican Republic—they both shared a deeper connection. It was not only in their affinity for hitting home runs, but in handling themselves in a modest and classy manner. When asked who he thought would win the home run race, Mark didn't hesitate when he said, "Wouldn't it be great if we ended up tied?"

The country felt the respect and love that these players openly shared for one another. What some had expected to be a bitter man-to-man competition, complete with the trash-talking and intimidation that are so prevalent in today's sports arena, had become a celebration of diversity, ability, and class. As the players took the field on September 6, fans across the nation were cheering for a new record to be made.

After just two more games, there would be a new chapter in the history of baseball.

TYING A RECORD

Hitting 60 or more home runs in a single season is the greatest goal in the game of baseball, a sport cherished as much for its many statistics as for its actual play. On September 5, 1998, Mark McGwire became the newest member of the most exclusive club in baseball when he cranked a 2-out pitch into the left-field bleachers, joining Roger Maris and Babe Ruth as the only players to have hit as many homers in a single season. Unlike the others, however, it took Mac only 142 games to reach this mark, whereas it took Ruth 154 games, and it wasn't until Maris's 159th game that he reached 60.

Mac crossed the mates John Mabry, after number 60 and was greeted h Ron Gant. They all Brian Jordan, rademark celebration of engaged in th popping tw ists against a teammate's before pla lly punching each other in the stomac Mark then pointed to the box seats behind the plate. "That was the owners'," he said. "I salute all of them."

After the game, Mark was mobbed by reporters, not only because of what he had just accomplished, but for what he was about to do. About Roger Maris at the top of the home run heap and whether he had thought much about breaking history, Mark said, "You are almost speechless when people put your name alongside his name. Hopefully, some day when I pass away, I'll get to meet him, and then I can truly find out what he was really like."

It would not be the first time that Mark would express his sincere feeling that his soul is somehow connected to Ruth and Maris. He was convinced that they were with him, watching over this grand drama. Regarding Maris, Mark offered, "What he did was absolutely tremendous. I mean, I can only imagine what he went through in New York City. I truly believe he is watching upstairs. I honestly believe he's there with me. I can't explain it. But I can feel it." After saying this, Mac then tapped his chest, as if to prove that Maris was in his heart.

Mark had little time to enjoy number 60 as the Chicago Cubs—and good friend Sammy Sosa—were coming into town. The world waited with excitement for this showdown.

After the pregame press conference, this game would start like any other. Mark would step into the batting cage at 11:53 A.M. for practice and, after bunting his customary first pitch, hit the first three pitches into the left-field bleachers, while Sammy Sosa watched from the corner of the batting cage. The St. Louis fans went wild. About a half hour later, Sosa would step in for batting practice; however, he received few cheers and little attention.

The fans finally began to show their appreciation when Sosa came to the plate in the top of the first. The crowd in St. Louis saluted the Dominican star with a standing ovation. Sosa stepped into the batter's box, then out, taking off his helmet to salute the crowd—which in turn cheered him louder. Unfortunately for Sammy, he would pop up on the third pitch for the last out—caught by none other than Mark McGwire.

In the bottom of the first, with two outs, Mark McGwire came to the plate. After taking a huge cut at a slider from Cubs pitcher Mike Morgan, his next pitch would be a fastball, high and out of the strike zone. At 1:22 P.M. Central Standard Time, Mark uncoiled, lining the ball down the left-field line. The ball hooked, but stayed fair by less than 10 feet, landing deep into left-field seats. Mark McGwire had hit his 61st home run of the season, tying Roger Maris's record set 37 years earlier.

Mark pumped his fists and started to cir-

before]. I thought he might try to hit 61 today. . . . What a birthday!"

His mother, Ginger, would later tell a reporter how she felt when she realized that her son had broken the record. "I was shaking. Crying and shaking. I don't think I ever saw him touch the plate."

Mark gave salutes, and blew kisses, and passed out hugs all over the dugout and stadium. He looked to the four sons and one daughter of the late Maris, who were seated near the field, and blew a kiss to the sky for their father.

Finally, with the fans still on their feet more than five minutes after Mac's record-tying home run, Mark jumped out of the dugout for a much anticipated curtain call. He then looked out to Sosa in left field and imitated his trademark post–home run gesture: two pounds on the chest. Then he pointed toward Sammy, adding a couple of more pounds of the heart for good measure.

In the postgame interview, Mark let the emotion of the moment run through him, unafraid to get misty and choked up at various times throughout. When asked about tying, and possibly breaking Roger Maris's record in the same stadium where Maris had finished his career, Mark simply said, "He is in my heart."

"What I have done is tied it," Mark said about the record. "I am one swing away from breaking it. When that is going to happen, if it is tomorrow, if it is the next day, we will just have to wait and see. But it has been a long, rough road."

Because the spectacle of this chase was so grand, baseball-collectible enthusiasts were eager to acquire anything to do with Mark's incredible year. The most prized possession, in the eyes of the collectors, was a home run baseball hit by Big Mac himself. If the ball happened to be home run number 60, 61, or 62, then it was very valuable. Soon an ethical question was on the minds of the American sports fans—if you were to catch a record-breaking home run, would you sell it (getting as much as one million dollars) or return it to the individual who hit the ball.

Deni Allen, who caught home run number 60 on Saturday, turned down numerous cash offers for the ball from a few collectors, for the opportunity to hit batting practice with the Cardinals, and season tickets for the following year. When 28-year-old Mike Davidson ended up with home run ball number 61, he knew that he was going to give it to McGwire, saying, "Because it would mean more to him and to baseball than it would to me, more than a million dollars." Instead, Mike asked for two autographed bats and two autographed jerseys, and prepared for numerous interviews with ESPN, Fox, and *Late Night with David Letterman.*

It was the second time in three days that the person who caught the home run ball didn't hesitate when given the choice between returning the ball to Mac or selling it for a lot of cash. It was yet another chapter of good faith and morality in the heartwarming saga that was surrounding Mark McGwire.

There would be another valuable baseball, the record-breaking number 62. As Mark had said in the postgame interview, "Just one more swing."

· 14 ·

ENTERING THE HISTORY BOOKS

On Tuesday afternoon, after Mark McGwire's record-tying home run the previous day, there was only one thing on the collective minds of St. Louis—that evening's game against the Chicago Cubs. McGwire mania was at an absolute peak, in large part due to the massive celebration of the previous day. Outside the stadium, tickets were going for between $300 and $500—for the bleachers! Better seats were going for much more. Everyone wanted to be at Busch Stadium that evening, in hopes of glimpsing Mac's record-breaking home run.

Outside the ballpark was a sea of television mobile vans and minicams, accompanied by numerous reporters shoving microphones in the faces of any passerby willing to discuss the magic of McGwire or what they would do if they ended up with the home run ball. The other major topic of the evening was basic—would this be the evening that Mark McGwire broke the 37-year-old record. This was a concern to many Cardinals fans, for if Mac were to go homerless in this game, the last game in a homestand, it would likely mean that his 62nd would come on the road, and that was something that St. Louis did not want to share. When Mark had been asked about this, he simply replied, "When it happens, it is up to the Man upstairs."

Earlier in the day, representatives from Baseball's Hall of Fame, in Cooperstown, New York, arrived with artifacts from Maris's historical efforts. Among them was the bat that he used to best Babe Ruth's record. Mark held the bat, rubbed it against his chest and said, "Roger, I hope you're with me tonight."

The massive media presence was there to capture history and beam it out to the rest of the world. The Fox Network recognized the spectacle this had become and chose to nationally broadcast the game, bumping the regularly scheduled programs to the following week. Mark McGwire was the television show of the evening!

Before the game began, Sammy and Mac came out to tape a spot for the "MTV Video Music Awards." When they read the cue cards, both laughed and exchanged high fives. After which, they parted ways and quietly went about their usual pregame warm up.

As had been the case all season, the stadium was nearly packed for Mac's batting practice. The raw display of power that the fans had come to expect did not disappoint, as Mark crushed 6 of 18 pitches into the stands. Sosa then took his cuts, in relative anonymity, especially compared to Mac. An hour later, the game began.

Mark appeared anxious as he grounded out on a 3-0 pitch in the first inning. After making an out in his first at bat, Mark strode to the plate with two outs in the bottom of the fourth inning. Cub's right-hander Steve Trachsel was on the mound. Mac jumped on the first pitch, sending a screaming liner that just cleared the fence down the left-field line. Home run! Mark became the most prolific single-season home run hitter in major league history.

Mark McGwire was officially the new Home Run King!

Home run number 62 came at 8:18 P.M., Central Time, and was estimated at 341 feet—Mark's shortest homer during a season of 500-foot-plus home runs. After connecting with the ball, Mark was not sure that it had enough juice to get over the fence, so he sprinted to first base thinking about a double. But because he had sent ball off of his bat with such velocity, it only took a split second for the ball to leave the ballpark. Mac threw his arms up. The crowd went wild.

Mark was excited. So excited in fact that as he approached first base, he was more interested in shaking hands with first-base coach Dave McKay than in touching first base. As he rounded first, Coach McKay reminded him to tag first, so Mark came back to touch it.

As he continued to round the diamond, he was congratulated by each of the Cubs infielders—first baseman Mark Grace, second baseman Mickey Morandini, shortstop Jose Hernandez, and third baseman Gary Gaetti, whom he embraced in a big hug.

Approaching home, Mark touched his chest and pointed to the sky in honor of Roger Maris. He then approached home to meet Cubs catcher Scott Servais, who reached out to shake Mac's hand, but McGwire hugged him, too. About his emotional trot around the bases, Mark would later comment, "I just hope I didn't act foolish. This is history."

After tagging home, officially scoring his record-breaking 62nd homer, Mark Mc-

Gwire picked up his son, Matt, who was waiting for him at home. Big Mac was then mobbed by his teammates. Even the Cardinals relief pitchers ran in from the bullpen to join in the celebration. Mark hugged manager Tony La Russa, he hugged the rest of the coaching staff, he hugged his teammates . . . there was hardly anyone on the field that wasn't hugged by Mark McGwire.

In a remarkable bit of sportsmanship displayed by two men, Sammy Sosa ran in from right field and embraced Mark McGwire. The fans, who had not stopped cheering since Mac's shot, got even louder as the two home run heroes hugged. Mark lifted Sammy into the air as Sosa patted McGwire on the back. The two then exchanged high fives and repeated the Cardinal's now-famous home run ritual. Mark then repeated Sammy's chest-pounding hand signal in a symbol of respect for Sammy and the Dominican Republic from which he came.

Mark's celebration was not over. He then went into the stands just adjacent to the Cardinal dugout to hug the six children of Maris, who were in attendance. Sharing a heartfelt moment, the Maris children were visibly moved, with tears in their eyes. After McGwire finished his celebrating with his teammates and the Maris family, someone handed him a microphone to address the sellout crowd, which was still standing and cheering.

"To all my family, my son, the Cubs, Sammy Sosa. It's unbelievable. Thank you, St. Louis."

After the game resumed—nine minutes later—Traschel struck out Ray Lankford to end the inning. As Mark took the field for the top of fifth inning, he received another thunderous cheer from the St. Louis fans, who were still buzzing from having witnessed history. Fifteen minutes after Mac's homer, Sammy Sosa came to the plate and got a standing ovation. The crowd then chanted "Sammy! Sammy!" Sosa ended up walking, to a cascade of booing fans who wanted to see Sammy display some heroics of his own. Neither Sammy nor Mark would homer for the rest of the game. The Cards ended up winning, 6–3.

For Mark, breaking the record was particularly moving since he had wanted to accomplish it at home. The Cardinals would follow this game with a five-game road trip, and Mac wanted to share the moment with the fans and city that embraced him since he came over from Oakland the previous season. "What a perfect way to end the homestand," Mac would later comment. "By hitting 62 for the city of St. Louis and all the fans. I truly wanted to do it here, and I did. Thank you, St. Louis."

Afterward, Mark would patiently and enthusiastically answer a series of questions about the historic home run from a throng of reporters (over 700 total) representing countries from all over the globe. Mark started off with a simple show of respect to the illustrious history of baseball: "Thanks to Babe, Roger, and everybody who's watching up there." About his chase to break the record he added, "It's put baseball back on the map as the sport. It's America's national pastime."

After he hit the home run, Mark said, "I don't remember anything after that. I was numb. I thought, 'I still have to play the game. Oh, my God. I can't believe this.'" He added, "It's such an incredible feeling. I can't believe I did it."

Since so much was made of the home run ball, and its overall value, it was interesting that Mark's home run never actually reached the stands. Just clearing the left field fence by two feet, it was ironic that this would be Mac's shortest home run of the entire season, but easily the most dramatic. The ball was recovered by Tim Forneris, a member of the Cardinals grounds crew, who quickly stuffed the ball into his shirt for safekeeping and ran onto the field with dozens of other jubilant groundskeepers.

Jonathan Hall

Tim Forneris returned the ball during the postgame ceremony, saying, "Mr. McGwire, I believe I have something of yours." The crowd cheered in support for another young individual who forgave personal financial gain in favor of doing the right thing. "It's not mine to begin with," the 22-year-old said. "McGwire just lost it, and I brought it home. I'm just a regular Joe." It was if Mark McGwire was instilling a sense of class and dignity into society, one fan at a time.

Long after Mark left for the press conference, roughly 40,000 of the 50,000 fans in attendance stayed for the postgame ceremony. The Cardinal organization honored Mark's phenomenal feat by presenting him with a cardinal-red 1962 Corvette in appreciation for his remarkable season. Mark would later ride around the perimeter of the stadium, receiving cheers and adulation from a capacity crowd that stayed long past the end of the game.

The headlines for the following day's *St. Louis Post-Dispatch* screamed,

"Unbelievable Class!" summing up the feeling in Busch Stadium that evening.

Mark McGwire had proven himself to be more than the greatest single-season home run hitter. He proved that he was a true gentleman who showed respect, class, and character at every opportunity. On September 8, 1998, Mark McGwire was a role model for this country, a true American hero.

· 15 ·
GETTING TO 70

Breaking the greatest record in the history of baseball required a great deal of concentration and focus, both on the playing field and off of it. Mac was used to the physical demands of playing baseball on a daily basis. He was unaccustomed to the increased demands of his time by the media who were all too eager to interview the new home run king. In the days that followed 62, Mark was asked every question imaginable from reporters across the world, and he was exhausted.

It is not uncommon for a player to take a few games off after he or she breaks a major record. A few days' rest gives a player time for interviews and allows the player much-needed rest and relaxation. But this would not be the case for Mark McGwire. He felt that as long as his teammates were out on the field, he should be playing alongside them. Besides, there was a home run race going on, and even though he had a comfortable lead over his friend Sammy (62 to 58), he did not want to take anything for granted.

But the stress and energy got to Mark a little bit. In the next six games that followed, Mark did not hit one over the fence. It was not quite a slump, but there was a sense among sportswriters and columnists that after break-ing the record of 61, Mac had let up a little bit, and was perhaps running out of steam.

Meanwhile, Sammy Sosa had picked up the pace where Mac had left off. Hitting 4 home runs in one week, Sammy eventually broke Roger Maris's record of 61 home runs, and tied Mark in spectacular fashion by hitting two home runs in one game, the second being a ninth-inning game-winner. With that effort, the nation's attention shifted back to Sammy, and the race for the home run title was in center stage.

While much had been made about the friendly rivalry between these two ballplayers, it was clear among the teammates and coaches of both players that they each wanted to win the home run title. Mark and Sammy continued to handle themselves with class and treat each other with respect, however, they remained fierce competitors.

As the 1998 baseball season wrapped up, the home run race captivated the nation's attention. Going back and forth, Mark and Sammy played a long-ball version of cat and mouse. Mark would hit 63, the next day Sammy would tie. On September 18, against the Milwaukee Brewers, Mac hit number 64, declaring that his post record-breaking mini-slump was over. Sammy went without a homer and Mark had found his groove again, almost as if he was rejuvenated by the competition. Some were saying that Mark was going to run away with the title.

Two days later, Mark launched number 65

into the deep left-field bleachers of Brewer Stadium. In his next at bat, he did it again, only this time there was a slight problem. Because a fan appeared to have reached over the fence and caught the baseball while it was in fair play, the umpire declared the hit a ground-rule double, and Mark had to stay on second base. After the hit was reviewed on videotape, it was clear that the ball had actually gone over the fence before being touched by the fan. Most everyone believed it should have been home run number 66, but it did not count as such.

When asked about the play, Mark calmly stated that he did indeed think that it was a home run. Mark understood that the call was just one in many breaks that go either for or against you in the game of baseball. Rather than get upset over the missed call, Mac seemed to shrug his shoulders and move on. He also felt pretty good that he had a two–home run lead over Sammy with just a week left in the season.

Three days later, also in Milwaukee, that

lead vanished with another two–home run game by Sammy Sosa. With only three games left in the season, Mark and Sammy were tied at 65 home runs. There was no way to tell who was going to win the home run race, as each player was capable of hitting multiple home runs in a game. The two ballplayers were putting on an incredible display of competition and power.

On Friday, September 25, Sammy struck the first blow with number 66. For only the second time all season, Sosa was in the lead. But without missing a beat, Mark answered with his own homer, just within an hour after Sammy's. Baseball had never been more exciting!

Entering the final two games of the season, Mac and Sammy were tied at 66 home runs. Sammy would be facing the Houston Astros (embroiled in a playoff race for the National League wild-card spot), while Mark would enjoy the friendly confines of Busch Stadium. Coming out of the weekend, Sammy still had 66. Mark McGwire had reached an unbelievable 70 home runs. That's nine home runs in front of Roger Maris's record. Big Mac didn't break the record—he shattered it!

Hitting 2 home runs in one game is a rare occurrence in baseball. Doing that in back-to-back games is even more exceptional. But hitting 5 home runs in 48 hours while the whole world is watching your every swing is truly phenomenal. While baseball historians will note that in 1998 Mark McGwire broke the single-season home run record, only the fans that were following his (and Sammy's) efforts during the last week will truly appreciate the excitement of what Mac accomplished in his final two games. Mark McGwire had proven that he is the greatest single-season home run hitter of all time.

· 16 ·

AN AMERICAN HERO

Hitting a 90-mile-per-hour fast-ball some four hundred feet is well documented as the most difficult accomplishment in all sports. To do it with consistency and power is even more challenging. It is harder still when the whole world is watching every step of the way. As *New York Times* columnist Murray Chass observed, the single-season home run record is like no other for "glamour, notoriety and its unyielding grip on the American consciousness."

The race for Roger Maris's record between Mark McGwire and Sammy Sosa could not have occurred at a better time for baseball, which had never fully recovered it popularity from the labor strike of three seasons prior. Baseball stadiums across the country were setting attendance records, in large part to see Ken Griffey, Jr., Sammy Sosa, or Mark McGwire come to town.

"You know," Mark said in a midseason interview, "the players are going to bring the fans back [to baseball]. How we play the game, what we do, that's what's going to do it. We're going to bring the fans back, and I think it's a start this year—whether it's what I'm doing or what the great players are doing."

When Mark McGwire hit his 62nd home run into the left-field bleachers of Busch Stadium, he entered the history books. Just as every other kid that grew up swinging a bat, Mark had heard of the legends of base-ball. "It still blows me away. It really does. Considering when I was a kid and all I ever wanted to do was pitch . . . then the next thing you know, they're talking about my name along with Babe Ruth, Maris, Mantle, down the line. It's overwhelming."

From the time that Mark started playing baseball as an 8-year-old, he had always been a reluctant home run hitter, preferring instead to pitch. It would take about 25 years for Mark to fully embrace the idea of himself as a home run hitter. Once he came to peace with that, the baseballs started flying. Mark's achievements are a testament to dedication, practice, and working out.

"I never dreamed of being in this position. I dreamed about being a big leaguer," Mark explained to the press. "Things happen for a reason. Hard work pays off."

Even though McGwire's single-season home run record will one day be broken, Mark entered the hearts and minds of the American people for a number of other reasons, far beyond his ability to smack a baseball further than anyone else.

He touched this country because of the character that he showed, through his successes and failures. He taught his fans, his family, and especially his son, an open love for the game of baseball. Without ever really saying a word, he showed how someone could withstand pressure, adversity, and competition with skill and grace. In his own way, Mark challenged his fans to be strong moral citizens. This is how America fell in love with Mark McGwire.

Statistics

#25, Mark McGwire
Position: First Base
Born: October 1, 1963, in Pomona, CA
Height: 6'5"
Weight: 225 lbs.
Bats: Right
Throws: Right
College: Southern Cal

Career Batting Statistics

Year	Team	G	AB	R	H	DO	TR	HR	RBI	BB	SO
1986	OAK	18	53	10	10	1	0	3	9	4	18
1987	OAK	151	557	97	161	28	4	49	118	71	131
1988	OAK	155	550	87	143	22	1	32	99	76	117
1989	OAK	143	490	74	113	17	0	33	95	83	94
1990	OAK	156	523	87	123	16	0	39	108	110	116
1991	OAK	154	483	62	97	22	0	22	75	93	116
1992	OAK	139	467	87	125	22	0	42	104	90	105
1993	OAK	27	84	16	28	6	0	9	24	21	19
1994	OAK	47	135	26	34	3	0	9	25	37	40
1995	OAK	104	317	75	87	13	0	39	90	88	77
1996	OAK	130	423	104	132	21	0	52	113	116	112
1997	OAK-STL	156	540	86	148	27	0	58	123	101	159
1998	STL	155	509	130	152	21	0	70	147	162	155
Totals:		1535	5131	941	1353	219	5	457	1130	1052	1259

Career Batting Statistics (continued)

Year	Team	SB	CS	OBP	SLG	AVG	TB	SF	SH	HBP	IBB	GIDP
1986	OAK	0	1	.259	.377	.189	20	0	0	1	0	0
1987	OAK	1	1	.370	.618	.289	344	8	0	5	8	6
1988	OAK	0	0	.352	.478	.260	263	4	1	4	4	15
1989	OAK	1	1	.339	.467	.231	229	11	0	3	5	23
1990	OAK	2	1	.370	.489	.235	256	9	1	7	9	13
1991	OAK	2	1	.330	.383	.201	185	5	1	3	3	13
1992	OAK	0	1	.385	.585	.268	273	9	0	5	12	10
1993	OAK	0	1	.467	.726	.333	61	1	0	1	5	0
1994	OAK	0	0	.413	.474	.252	64	0	0	0	3	3
1995	OAK	1	1	.441	.685	.274	217	6	0	11	5	9
1996	OAK	0	0	.467	.73	.312	309	1	0	8	16	14
1997	OAK-STL	3	0	.393	.646	.274	349	7	0	9	16	9
1998	STL	1	0	.470	.752	.299	383	4	0	6	28	8
	Totals:	11	8	.391	.576	.264	2953	65	3	63	114	123

Career Fielding Statistics

Year	Team	Posn	G	GS	TC	PO	A	E	DP	FLD%
1986	OAK	3B	16	15	36	10	20	6	1	0.833
1987	OAK	1B	145	141	1273	1173	90	10	91	0.992
1987	OAK	3B	8	5	16	2	11	3	0	0.813
1987	OAK	OF	3	2	1	1	0	0	0	1.000
1988	OAK	1B	154	146	1325	1228	88	9	118	0.993
1988	OAK	OF	1	0	0	0	0	0	0	—
1989	OAK	1B	141	139	1290	1170	114	6	122	0.995
1990	OAK	1B	154	150	1429	1329	95	5	126	0.997
1991	OAK	1B	152	142	1296	1191	101	4	120	0.997
1992	OAK	1B	139	136	1195	1118	71	6	118	0.995
1993	OAK	1B	25	25	211	197	14	0	20	1.000
1994	OAK	1B	40	37	329	307	18	4	26	0.988
1995	OAK	1B	91	88	851	775	64	12	65	0.986
1996	OAK	1B	109	107	983	913	60	10	118	0.990
1997	OAK-STL	1B	151	149	1424	1323	94	7	129	0.995
1998	STL	1B	152	152	1434	1326	96	12	128	0.992

About the Author

Jonathan Hall has contributed to many youth-culture magazines, including *Spin* and *Vibe*, and to numerous Web sites. Before writing, Jonathan spent eight years working as a camp counselor at Hidden Valley Children's Camp and Maine Teen Camp.

Jonathan is also the author of Archway's *Kobe Bryant: A Biography*.